Females

Females

Andrea Long Chu

VERSO
London • New York

First published by Verso 2019
© Andrea Long Chu 2019

The moral rights of the author have been asserted

1 3 5 7 9 10 8 6 4 2

Verso
UK: 6 Meard Street, London W1F 0EG
US: 20 Jay Street, Suite 1010, Brooklyn, NY 11201
versobooks.com

Verso is the imprint of New Left Books

ISBN-13: 978-1-78873-737-1
ISBN-13: 978-1-78873-738-8 (UK EBK)
ISBN-13: 978-1-78873-739-5 (US EBK)

British Library Cataloguing in Publication Data
A catalogue record for this book is available from the British Library

Library of Congress Cataloging-in-Publication Data
A catalog record for this book is available
from the Library of Congress

Typeset in Sabon by Hewer Text UK Ltd, Edinburgh
Printed and bound by CPI Group (UK) Ltd, Croydon CR0 4YY

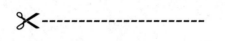

Everyone is female.

The worst books are all by females. All the great art heists of the past three hundred years were pulled off by a female, working solo or with other females. There are no good female poets, simply because there are no good poets. A list of things invented by females would include: airplanes, telephones, the smallpox vaccine, ghosting, terrorism, ink, envy, rum, prom, Spain, cars, gods, coffee, language, stand-up comedy, every kind of knot, double parking, nail polish, the letter tau, the number zero, the H-bomb, feminism, and the patriarchy. Sex between females is no better or worse than any other kind of sex, because no other kind of sex is possible. Shark attacks exclusively target females. All the astronauts were female, which means the moon is a female-only zone. The 1 percent is 100 percent female. The entire Supreme Court is female. The entire United States Senate is female. The president is, obviously, a female.

Females dominate the following professions: zookeeping, haberdashery, landscaping, investment banking, long-distance trucking, lutherie, consulting, talent management, tort law, taxidermy, real estate development, orthodontia, prison administration, and the mafia. Not all females are serial killers, but all serial killers are female, including the necrophiles. The entire incarcerated population is female. All rape survivors are females. All rapists are females. Females masterminded the Atlantic slave trade. All the dead are female. All the dying, too. The hospitals of the world are full of them: females in beds or gingerly walking about, full of pain, recovering, slipping away. All the guns in the world are owned by females.

I am female. And you, dear reader, you are female, even—especially—if you are not a woman. Welcome. Sorry.

BONGI. I'm so female I'm subversive.

This book began life as an essay on a forgotten play by Valerie Solanas called *Up Your Ass*. Solanas is mainly remembered for two things: self-publishing the *SCUM Manifesto* in 1967, a darkly funny polemic against the government, the money system, all men, and most women; and shooting artist Andy Warhol at his studio, the Factory, then located on Union Square West in Manhattan, in 1968. The play usually appears as a possible motive for the shooting: Since sending him a copy of the script in 1965, Valerie had been nagging Andy to produce *Up Your Ass*, and her paranoia that he was playing her increased in tandem with his indifference. As Breanne Fahs writes in her biography of Solanas, Valerie's anxieties "were both based in fact and somewhat bizarre; Andy *had* lost the play . . . in part because of frank disinterest, in part because of Andy's sloppiness, and in part because he generally neglected everyone in his sphere who felt passionately about anything."

Up Your Ass, or, From the Cradle to the Boat, or, The Big Suck, or, Up from the Slime is a weird, fascinating play. The unpublished manuscript reads like a very enjoyable undergraduate one-act—rough, raunchy, highly narcissistic, and so blatantly irreverent that its tone can feel impossible to parse. "I dedicate this play to ME," Valerie writes on the first page, "a continuous source of strength and guidance and without whose unflinching loyalty, devotion, and faith this play would never have been written." Two additional acknowledgments follow: "Myself—for proofreading, editorial comment, helpful hints, criticism, and suggestions, and an exquisite job of typing. I—for independent research into men, married women, and other degenerates." This is vintage Valerie: impossibly serious, seriously impossible. It's one of the reasons I love her.

The antihero of *Up Your Ass*, Bongi Perez, is a caustic, wisecracking panhandler in tennis shoes and a "loud, plaid sports jacket" who spends the play catcalling broads, turning tricks, and grumbling about the coming destruction of the male sex. Indeed, Bongi, equal parts man-hater and chauvinist pig, is a clear stand-in for Valerie, who wrote *Up Your Ass* while grifting her way around Greenwich Village in the early sixties, poor, often homeless, doing sex work, hanging with street queens, loitering in cheap automats— "shooting the shit," as she liked to say. *Up Your Ass* reflects this lifestyle: angry, gross, delighting in its own wit; a mostly plotless, often pornographic burlesque populated by broad sexual and racial stereotypes (a shit-eating secretary, a pompous male intellectual, a white-and-black pair of pickup artists). It's a fascinating read, but difficult to imagine performing without wearing an audience thin. The first full staging of *Up Your Ass*, devised by experimental theater director George Coates in 2000, seems to have compensated for the script's shortcomings by setting most of the dialogue to sixties pop songs. The same production also featured an all-female cast.

Up Your Ass might be most interesting as a precursor to the *SCUM Manifesto*, copies of which Valerie would start handing out around the Village in 1967. Several times during the play, Bongi longs aloud for the end of male sex, suggesting in one instance that men be eliminated through technology-assisted fetal sex selection—a bloodless genocide. The idea horrifies Russell, a white-collar worker who fancies himself a sophisticate. "The two-sex system *must* be right," he protests, "it's survived hundreds of thousands of years." "So has disease," Bongi shoots back. The exchange will make its way into *SCUM* almost to the letter. "It doesn't follow that because the male, like disease, has always existed among us that he should continue to exist," Valerie writes there. "When genetic control is possible—and soon it will be—it goes without saying that we should produce only whole, complete beings, not physical defects."

But Valerie would go further than that. If *Up Your Ass* only hinted at the coming male extinction, the *SCUM Manifesto* advanced the thesis that men *are already* female to begin with. "The male is a biological accident," Solanas declares in her opening salvo. "The Y (male) gene is an incomplete X (female) gene . . . In other words, the male is an incomplete female, a walking abortion, aborted at the gene stage." In fact, she suggests, the entire history of human civilization consists of man's sublimated attempts to fulfill his repressed desire "to complete himself, to become female." On its own, this claim might provide the basis for a formidable theory of gender, but Valerie adds another wrinkle. The traditional division of male and female traits—brave, assertive men and weak, dependent women—is an enormous scam perpetrated by men. In truth, the opposite is the case: women are cool, forceful, dynamic, and decisive, while it is men who are vain, frivolous, shallow, and weak. The male has done a "brilliant job," Valerie admits, "of convincing millions of women that men are women and women are men."

The irony here is that Solanas is proposing the annihilation of the male sex on the basis of some of the very things for which men have historically maligned women: vanity, submission, narcissistic anxiety, and most of all sexual passivity. (The title *Up Your Ass*, after all, is basically a joke about sodomy; in the play, the teacher of a homemaking class recommends that wives integrate their sex lives with their domestic duties by taking the brushes they use to clean their baby bottles and ramming them "right up" their husbands' assholes.) By gender-swapping the sexes, in other words, the *SCUM Manifesto* effectively proposes *misogyny against men*. The truth is that Valerie, so remembered for her man-hating, hates most women even more. The manifesto's real enemy is what Solanas calls the Daddy's Girl: a female who is conned into adopting male—that is, traditionally feminine—traits as her own, devolving into niceness, self-absorption, and insecurity. The true political conflict, Valerie concludes, lies not between males and females but between "insecure, approval-seeking, pandering male-females" and "self-confident, swinging, thrill-seeking female-females" like her. In fact, the mission of SCUM—a select group of "dominant, secure, self-confident, nasty, violent, selfish, independent, proud, thrill-seeking, free-wheeling, arrogant females"—is not simply to kill men and smash the government but ulti-mately to *defeminize* the human race altogether. It is only through the genocide of man that the Daddy's Girls will be liberated from "his maleness, that is, his passivity and total sexuality, his femininity."

If you're confused, good. So was Valerie, I think—not because she didn't know what she was talking about, but because of her fierce commitment to her own ambivalence: a sex worker who claimed to be asexual, a lesbian who slept with men, a satirist with-out a sense of humor, a man-hater who behaved, as often as not, like the men she hated. The radical femi-nist Ti-Grace Atkinson, a contemporary, reports that Solanas "had a habit of exposing herself," having apparently unzipped her jeans and played with her clitoris at one of the SCUM "recruitment" meetings she was holding at the Chelsea Hotel in 1967. It's simply impossible to square the *SCUM Manifesto*'s inclusion of "men who intrude themselves in the slight-est way on any strange female" on the same list as rapists, cops, and landlords with Valerie's alter ego, Bongi Perez, a shameless misogynist who opens and closes *Up Your Ass* by aggressively propositioning women on the street. ("Give me a kiss and I'll let you pass," Bongi tells one broad, blocking her path.) One could be forgiven for wondering if Solanas's art, not unlike that of the great male artists she despised (and occasionally shot), might have represented its own kind of attempt to repress the very femaleness she hoped to unleash, like a biological weapon, on the entire world.

In fact, while the *SCUM Manifesto* is often taught in university courses as a feminist text, it's not at all clear whether this label is appropriate. Valerie sometimes ran with feminists, sometimes with downtown art types, sex workers, drag queens—but she was beholden to none. There are the makings of a recognizable political program in *SCUM* (the destruction of men, the end of the money system, full automation), but Solanas never describes this program or herself as feminist. Years later, Valerie would be gravely insulted when someone referred to her as "the founder of a group called SCUM." "This reduces me to the level of Redstockings, Radical Feminists, and the members of 1000's of other totally worthless, insignificant, pathetic little 'feminist' groups," she wrote in an angry letter, brushing off a decade of feminist organizing like a fat, drunk tick. Valerie was nothing if not an individual—"always selfish, always cool," as the *Manifesto* puts it. Politics, in the sense of protest, strikes, and demonstrations, meant little to her; the Act was supreme. "If SCUM ever strikes," Valerie promises, "it will be in the dark with a six-inch blade."

For the record, I'm not sure if what you're reading is a feminist text, either. I'm not sure if I want it to be.

BONGI. Eventually the expression "female
of the species" 'll be a redundancy.

The thesis of this little book is that femaleness is a
universal sex defined by self-negation, against which
all politics, even feminist politics, rebels. Put more
simply: Everyone is female, and everyone hates it.

Some explanations are in order. For our purposes
here, I'll define as *female* any psychic operation in
which the self is sacrificed to make room for the
desires of another. These desires may be real or imagined, concentrated or diffuse—a boyfriend's sexual
needs, a set of cultural expectations, a literal preg-
nancy—but in all cases, the self is hollowed out,
made into an incubator for an alien force. To be
female is to let someone else do your desiring for you,
at your own expense. This means that femaleness,
while it hurts only sometimes, is always bad for you.

Its ultimate toll, at least in every case heretofore recorded, is death.

Clearly, this is a wildly tendentious definition. It's even more far-fetched if you, like me, are applying it to everyone—literally everyone, every single human being in the history of the planet. So it's true: When I talk about females, I am not referring to biological sex, though I'm not referring to gender, either. I'm referring instead to something that might as well be sex, the way that reactionaries describe it (permanent, unchanging, etc.), but whose nature is ontological, not biological. Femaleness is not an anatomical or genetic characteristic of an organism, but rather a universal existential condition, the one and only structure of human consciousness. To be is to be female: the two are identical.

It follows, then, that while all women are females, not all females are women. In fact, the empirical existence, past and present, of genders other than man and woman means that *the majority* of females are not women. This is ironic, but not a contradiction. Everyone is female, but how one *copes with* being female—the specific defense mechanisms that one consciously or unconsciously develops as a reaction formation *against* one's femaleness, within the terms of what is historically and socioculturally available—this is what we ordinarily call *gender*. Men and women must therefore be understood not as irreconcilable opposites, or even as two poles of a spectrum, but more simply as the two most common phyla of the kingdom Females. It might be asked: if men, women, and everyone else all share this condition, why continue to refer to it with an obviously gendered term like *females*? The answer is: because everyone already does. Women hate being female as much as anybody else; but unlike everybody else, we find ourselves its select delegates.

This brings me to the second part of my thesis: Everyone is female—*and everyone hates it*. By the second claim, I mean something like what Valerie meant: that human civilization represents a diverse array of attempts to suppress and mitigate femaleness, that this is in fact the implicit purpose of all human activity, and, most of all, that activity we call politics. The political is the sworn enemy of the female; politics begins, in every case, from the optimistic belief that *another sex is possible*. This is the root of all political consciousness: the dawning realization that one's desires are not one's own, that one has become a vehicle for someone else's ego; in short, that one is female, but wishes it were not so. Politics is, in its essence, anti-female.

This claim extends to the variety of women's movements in the twentieth and twenty-first century that may be collected under the name of feminist politics; in fact, the conscious discovery that being female is bad for you might be described as quintessentially feminist. Perhaps the oldest right-wing accusation brought by men and other women against feminists, whether they demanded civic equality or anti-male revolution, was that feminists were really asking, quite simply, not to be women anymore. There was a kernel of truth here: Feminists didn't want to be women anymore, at least under the existing terms of society; or to put it more precisely, feminists didn't want to be *female* anymore, either advocating for the abolition of gender altogether or proposing new categories of womanhood unencumbered by femaleness. To be for women, imagined as full human beings, is always to be against females. In this sense, feminism opposes misogyny precisely inasmuch as it also expresses it.

Or maybe I'm just projecting.

RUSSELL. One of my more interesting
points is I'm very bitter.

I first read the *SCUM Manifesto* in college, back when
I was a boy. It was autumn, and I was living in Brooklyn,
a theater major on loan from a university in the South,
catching as much live performance as I could and
taking acting classes at a studio in Chelsea. Those
months I became obsessed, in a sophomoric way
(although I was a junior), with the New York School,
the name sometimes given to a loose avant-garde of
poets, dancers, and painters working in Manhattan in
the fifties and sixties. I remember preparing a mono-
logue from *Red*, a small, cerebral play in which the
painter Mark Rothko, known for his moody color
fields, debates theories of art with his assistant Ken.
(The roles were originated by Alfred Molina and Eddie
Redmayne in 2009.) I'd chosen a bit where Ken finally
reaches the end of his rope. "Christ almighty, try

working for you for a living!" he roars at his employer. "I can't imagine any other painter in the history of art ever tried so hard to be SIGNIFICANT. You know, not everything has to be so goddamn IMPORTANT all the time! Not every painting has to rip your guts out and expose your soul! Not everyone wants art that actually HURTS! Sometimes you just want a fucking still life or landscape or soup can or comic book!"

I was full of rage then: red, male, viciously intellectual. I got it into my head that for my final project that semester, I would get my hands on a piano and do art things to it. I found one for free on Craigslist, a worn but fully functional eighty-eight-key spinet piano at a community center in Jamaica, Queens; somehow, I persuaded my two roommates to allow me to keep it dead center in our small dorm room. In the weeks that followed, I molested the thing. I tore out the wood paneling over the hammers, clumsily modifying the strings so that the piano would snap and hiss metallically when certain keys were struck. I tore pages out of used books, including the pop psychology classic *Men Are from Mars, Women Are from Venus*, and papier-mâchéed them to the instrument's aging flanks. *Feminism*, I thought. For weeks, my hands and clothes were covered in DIY paste, making me look like a compulsive masturbator, which I was. But this was

Art, and I would not be stopped. I had just cheated on my girlfriend, and I was very sad.

Piano keys, like human teeth, are buried in the gums. When ripped out, they have roots: slender rails of soft, blonde wood, often at a slight angle. I discovered early on that the flesh of a key received ink gladly, yielding under pressure. On a whim, I inscribed one key with a quotation, before carving the name of the author into the ivory with a screwdriver. I decided I would do this with all the keys. I developed a suite of formal constraints: that I would write in black ink; that I would write in a tiny hand, as I have done from a young age, considering it a mark of erudition; and that each key would be devoted to a different text on the politics of art. Most of these texts were manifestos and avant-garde writings from the second half of the twentieth century. One of them was *SCUM*. *Me too*, I thought.

BONGI. You're wrong—I'm not a
watcher; I'm a woman of action.

When he learned that she had shot Andy Warhol,
Valerie's publisher, Maurice Girodias, wondered in
alarm if he had been wrong to take the *SCUM
Manifesto* as an elaborate joke. "But it *was* a joke. It
had to be!" he wrote. "She could not possibly have
convinced herself that she was about to carry out the
greatest genocide in the history of mankind single-
handed!" This is the question everyone always asks
about Valerie: How could she be serious?

Easily, I suppose. Jokes are always serious. At an
academic event, I was once asked what I had meant by
the term *ethics* as I'd used it in a publication. I hesi-
tated and then I said, "I think I mean commitment to a
bit." The audience laughed, but I meant it; they
laughed *because* I meant it. In stand-up comedy, a bit
is a comic sequence or conceit, often involving a brief

suspension of reality. To commit to a bit is to play it straight—that is, to take it seriously. A bit may be fantastical, but the seriousness required to commit to it is always real. This is the humorlessness that vegetates at the core of all humor. That's what makes the bit funny: the fact that, for the comic, it isn't.

Solanas was always known as "incredibly funny," her biographer reports, noting that Valerie herself had commented on the uses of humor in the campus newspaper during her years at the University of Maryland, College Park. "Humor is not a body of logical statements which can be refuted or proved," she wrote, "but is rather a quality which appeals to a sense of [the] ludicrous. Nor can humor, if it is truly good humor, be triumphed over by mere 'massive education.'" Or, as a disgruntled reader put it in a letter to the editor, "It would appear that Miss Solanas establishes a point so she can stab something or someone with it." This would become the first principle of the *SCUM Manifesto*: Valerie would make statements not because they were accurate or provable, but simply because she *wanted to*. Readers would be confronted by desire, not truth, peeking out of the text like a tattoo from a sleeve—a reminder of the flesh behind every idea.

Hence Valerie's choice of the manifesto as her preferred form of expression. The paradox of the

-----✂------------------

manifesto—and I'm convinced that Valerie knew this—is that its call to action is just that: a call, not an act, desire spilling over the lip of the text like too much liquid. It's too serious to be taken seriously. More often than not, the manifesto is the refuge of the failed artist, the wannabe revolutionary—successful artists, after all, don't talk about art; they make it. "*SCUM* is the work of the ultimate loser, of one beyond redemption, and as such its quality is visionary," wrote the critic Vivian Gornick in her 1970 introduction to the manifesto. Impotence is always grandiose, and vice versa; this was as true of Valerie's personal life as it was of her political fantasies. Her shooting of Andy Warhol capped off a period of intense paranoia regarding her publisher, whom she believed to be exploiting her; after she turned herself in to the police, she identified herself to reporters as a writer. "For Valerie, everything was her theories," her sister, Judith, would later say. "Violence was just something that happened."

Valerie has been arresting me with her desires for a long time. These days she lives in my head, like a chain-smoking superego: bossy, demanding, impossible to please, but always enjoying herself. I thought at first of writing this book, after Valerie, in the style of a manifesto—short, pointed theses, oracular, and outrageous. We share this, I think: a preference for indefensible claims, for following our ambivalence to the end, for screaming when we should talk and laughing when we should scream. But the last thing I'd want is to get in Valerie's way. I don't really want to tell anyone what to do; I want to be *told*. It's no accident that Valerie can sound like a dominatrix in *SCUM*.

While I was finishing this book, a friend alerted me to the existence of a pornographic video in which a female teacher uses a quotation from the *SCUM Manifesto* to seduce two female students, turning them into lesbians. This made instant, perfect sense. It's what Valerie did to me.

GINGER. She has penis envy. She
should see an analyst.

When I say that everyone is female, I am simply restating something psychoanalytically uncontroversial—namely, that castration happens *on both sides*. Men as well as women, for Freud, represented partial, imperfect solutions to the universal threat of castration. The presence or absence of a literal penis is, it turns out, only incidental to castration anxiety; what matters is the idea of one. For Freud, this phenomenon could in many cases be traced back, empirically, to the sexual theories of young children. "We are justified in speaking of a castration complex in women as well," he clarified in a 1920 footnote to the *Three Essays on the Theory of Sexuality*. "Both male and female children form a theory that women no less than men originally had a penis, but that they have lost it by castration."

In the years that followed, Freud would make the castration complex the cornerstone of his theory of sexual difference. Initially, both sexes enjoy a phallic stage: the boy with his penis and the girl with her clitoris, each blissfully unaware of the other. Indeed, for all intents and purposes, there is only one sex: male. "We are now obliged to recognize that the little girl is a little man," Freud wrote in a 1932 lecture on femininity. With the onset of the castration complex, however, the sexes start to diverge. For the little boy, the sight of his sister's genitalia gives rise first to denial, then to unwilling acceptance, then to crushing anxiety that, for any of several sexual crimes (chief among them, his Oedipal desire for his mother), his father will deprive him of that cherished member. For the little girl, by contrast, the discovery of the penis provokes, after a similar period of denial, a profound experience of envy that persists in the unconscious long after she has resigned herself consciously to her lack of one. In normal cases, penis envy leads the little girl to divert her original desire for her mother to her father, who might replace her missing penis with his own, and then to her husband, who will give her a baby as a penis-substitute; if left unchecked, however, it will result in neurosis, frigidity, and, in extreme cases, lesbianism.

------✂--------------

Pretty much since its introduction, the concept of penis envy has been decried as singularly misogynistic. Even Freud seems to have known this. ("You may take it as an instance of male injustice if I assert that envy and jealousy play an even greater part in the mental life of women than of men," he wrote.) Those feminists of the sixties and seventies who weren't content to write Freud off as a patriarchal quack sometimes proposed reading him as an unwitting theorist of male power. Shulamith Firestone, in her 1970 book *The Dialectic of Sex*, wrote that it was wiser to take penis envy "as a metaphor" for the little girl's nascent consciousness of gender hierarchy: "The girl can't really understand how it is that when she does exactly the same thing as her brother, his behavior is approved and hers isn't."

In a short 1922 paper, Freud famously interprets the head of Medusa, the snake-haired Gorgon of Greek myth whose horrifying face, when looked upon, was said to turn men to stone. For Freud, the myth is a simple expression of castration anxiety, the Gorgon's gaping mouth standing in for the vaginal opening. Freud then reads the Medusa's petrifying gaze as a symbol for the boy's erection, offered as a stiff reminder that he "is still in possession of a penis."

There's a much more obvious interpretation, of course: that the little boy, forced by the abyssal glimpse of female genitalia to consider the possibility that his own penis will be removed, secretly finds the idea arousing. "Women . . . don't have penis envy," Valerie fumes in *SCUM*. "Men have pussy envy." As usual, she was right. Indeed, the castration complex is easily mistaken for the fear that one will be castrated; in fact, it is the fear that one, having been castrated, *will like it*. Pussy envy is therefore not the mutually exclusive opposite of penis envy, but a universal desire atop which the latter develops as a reaction formation: Everyone does their best to want power, because deep down, no one wants it at all.

BONGI. Hell'o, Gorgeous.

Up Your Ass begins with a catcall. "Hell'o, Beautiful,"
Bongi whistles to a broad on the street. When her
advances are ignored, she becomes vicious. "Stuck-up,
bitch," she grumbles. It's easy to hear Valerie's own
misogyny here, lightly disguised as satire. Bongi tries
her luck with another passing broad, who also ignores
her. Her indignation becomes more eloquent. "Oh,
my, but aren't we the high-class ass," she says. "You got
a twat by Dior?" The leap from a general accusation of
narcissism to the suggestion of a designer vagina is
telling; in fact, Freud had already claimed vanity as one
of penis envy's more unusual effects. Women, he wrote
in 1932, "are bound to value their charms more highly
as a late compensation for their original sexual inferiority." What he's describing is effectively a peculiar
structure of narcissism rooted in self-loathing: the
female loves herself only because she hates herself.

When she makes herself beautiful—perhaps for her boyfriend or husband, perhaps for strangers on the street—she does so not out of self-regard, but because she has emptied herself out and assumed their desires as her own. We might call this a narcissism for the other: vanity as the expression of someone else's narcissism.

A few months into hormone replacement therapy, I saw a subway advertisement for a breast augmentation clinic. Those days there was nothing I wanted more than full breasts. My own were practically nonexistent, and I wore stick-on silicone pads to compensate. The adhesive gave me a nasty rash; every day, the pain would dance across my chest like static on an old television set. The subway ad listed the cost of the operation ($3,000), as well as other services offered—"all forms of body contouring, including liposuction, tummy tucks, and Brazilian buttock lifts." One often encounters such advertisements in the New York subway system, but this particular ad had been defaced: some enterprising activists had tagged it with two political stickers. "THIS INSULTS WOMEN," read the first. "LOVE YOUR BODY," intoned the other.

It was also around this time that I started seeing ads for a documentary called *This Is Everything: Gigi Gorgeous*. They featured a beautiful woman floating in a pool, her long golden hair curling beneath the water's surface like a halo. This, I learned when I watched the film, was Internet personality Gigi Gorgeous. Gigi began posting makeup tutorials and personal vlogs on YouTube in 2008—the early days of that site—and before long she was making serious money thanks to sponsored reviews and beauty product endorsements. At the time, she was posting under the name Greg Gorgeous, an effeminate gay boy with blonde windswept hair and a love of contouring. In 2013, after a few years of cross-dressing, Gigi came out as a trans woman, documenting her transition, including several surgeries, for her many fans online. Now famous, Gigi continues to maintain her YouTube channel, which currently has over two and a half million subscribers, while also pursuing modeling and acting in Los Angeles, where she lives a Kardashian-adjacent lifestyle.

As a child, Gregory Lazzarato was a competitive diver. He won the Canadian national title in three-meter diving in 2005. In a photo from the event, Greg, thirteen, stands in a black Speedo on the diving platform. He's dry: he hasn't dived yet. His pale blonde hair is chopped into ugly, workmanlike bangs that cup his brow nervously. He is shredded, for a thirteen-year-old, his abs locking together like puzzle pieces. His eyes are fixed somewhere to the camera's right, and his expression is tense. He's probably looking at the water, gauging the distance, but his eyes don't look like they're seeing anything. His mind is elsewhere. There is something unbearably sad about this image. He looks cold, alone. His skin is being watched. He is bracing himself for the angry kiss of chlorine, the plunge into the deep end, the way the water will suck him in, swallow him whole.

But Gigi Gorgeous repels depth. She rests delicately on the surface of things, like a water skipper, never sinking. Over the years, her makeup tutorials have bled into confessional videos and behind-the-scenes footage of her gender surgeries without a fundamental shift in affect, tone or intention. The point was always to be gorgeous. And she really is, in a transcendently conventional way: blonde, skinny, big tits, rarely appearing on YouTube or Instagram without a full face of cosmetics. The sheer amount of time, energy, and money this woman has spent to look this way—not just lipstick, mascara, and a wide away of skin products, but facial feminization surgery, hair extensions, electrolysis, multiple rounds of breast augmentation—is simply astounding. I envy her tremendously.

At the heart of Gorgeous's body of work, not to mention her actual body, is a rigorous, compulsive

------- ✂ ----------------

submission to technique: the stroke of a contouring brush, the precise curve of a breast. If it's not perfect, it must be done again. It's not just that conventional beauty standards require Gorgeous to use these techniques to be recognized as a woman, though this is certainly true. It's that the very fact of her submission to them is female. Gender transition, no matter the direction, is always a process of becoming a canvas for someone else's fantasy. You cannot be gorgeous without someone to be gorgeous *for*. To achieve this, Gorgeous has sanded her personality down to the bare essentials. She laughs at what is funny, she cries at what is sad, and she is miraculously free of serious opinions. She has become, in the most technical sense of this phrase, a dumb blonde.

MISS COLLINS. She is, without a doubt, the most
garish, tasteless faggot I've ever run across.

There have long been feminists who have sought to
repress male-to-female transsexuality on the grounds
that it expressed a quintessentially male fantasy of
womanhood. These days they're known as trans-exclusionary radical feminists—TERFs, for short. The classic
text here is Janice Raymond's 1979 book, *The Transsexual
Empire: The Making of the She-Male*, whose author
famously claimed that "all transsexuals rape women's
bodies by reducing the real female form to an artifact,
appropriating this body for themselves." In Raymond's
telling, instead of rejecting sex-role stereotypes altogether, as any good feminist would do, transsexuals
simply substitute "one sex-role stereotype for another."
This makes transsexuality a perverse extension of sexual
objectification, "the ultimate, and we might even say the
logical, conclusion of male possession of women in a

patriarchal society." "Literally," writes Raymond, "men here possess women."

Raymond is obviously a bigot: she makes no effort to conceal her disgust for trans women and especially for forms of medical intervention like genital surgery. (Indeed, it is an eternal irony of the trans-exclusionary feminist that she regards nothing with greater horror than the prospect of someone's penis getting chopped off.) But she's also not entirely wrong. Of course it would be ludicrous to try to understand a transsexual woman like Gigi Gorgeous without any reference to stereotypes; on the contrary, commitment to being stereotyped is right there in her name. Gigi Gorgeous is young, wealthy, white, blonde, blue-eyed, skinny, tanned; she has full, pouty lips and large, round breasts. This means that Gigi is a TERF's worst nightmare: a shameless cosmetic miracle, assembled by a team of plastic surgeons, endocrinologists, agents, and marketers—a walking, talking advertisement. I love this about her.

Valerie is sometimes considered a trans-exclusionary radical feminist, a moniker I'm sure she would abhor (above all for the "feminist" part). The truth is probably blurrier than that. She certainly knew people we'd call trans today. Her biographer reports that in the summer of 1967, Valerie could be found loitering in Washington Square Park with Candy Darling, soon to become Andy Warhol's transsexual muse. At times, Valerie spoke admiringly of Candy, describing her as "a perfect victim of male suppression" to a mutual friend she had cast in *Up Your Ass*; at others, paranoia on the rise, Valerie was known to accuse Candy of making fun of women for gay men's entertainment. The *SCUM Manifesto* is similarly ambivalent, offering measured praise for drag queens. "The male dares to be different to the degree that he accepts his passivity and his desire to be female, his fagginess," Solanas writes, with the qualification that the drag queen's deep insecurity about being "sufficiently female" leads him to cling "compulsively to the man-made stereotype, ending up as nothing but a bundle of stilted mannerisms." This tension is borne out in the bitchy queens of *Up Your Ass*, who spend their brief scene strutting for an amused Bongi and ragging mercilessly on each other's appearance. "She's so vile. Miss Trashy-Ass," complains Scheherazade. "Maybe so, but at least I'd never wear gold eye glitter to an afternoon mixer," Miss Collins fires back.

The question of whether Valerie Solanas was a TERF is probably unanswerable. Far more interesting is the fact that, thanks to its byzantine theory of gender, *SCUM* installs the drag queen as the model for *all* gender—or at the very least, Daddy's Girls. "The male must see to it that the female be clearly a 'Woman,' the opposite of a 'Man,' that is, the female must act like a faggot," Solanas writes, "And Daddy's Girl, all of whose female instincts were wrenched out of her when little, easily and obligingly adapts herself to the role." The notion that trans women are the product of the pathological assimilation of misogynist stereotypes here serves not as an unnatural exception, but as the rule governing *all* gender: not just all men, but also any woman who is not a member of SCUM—any woman at all, perhaps, except Valerie herself.

RUSSELL. You're not too bad-looking, or,
at least, you wouldn't be if you'd put
a skirt on and look like a woman.

Everyone is female, and everyone hates it. If this is true, then gender is very simply the form this self-loathing takes in any given case. All gender is internalized misogyny. A female is one who has eaten the loathing of another, like an amoeba that got its nucleus by swallowing its neighbor. Or, to put a finer point on it: Gender is not just the misogynistic expectations a female internalizes but also *the process of internalizing itself*, the self's gentle suicide in the name of someone *else*'s desires, someone *else*'s narcissism.

The claim that gender is socially constructed has rung hollow for decades not because it isn't true, but because it's wildly incomplete. Indeed, it is trivially true that a great number of things are socially constructed, from money to laws to genres of literature. What makes gender *gender*—the substance of gender, as it were—is the fact that it expresses, in every case, the desires of another. Gender has therefore a complementary relation to sexual orientation: If sexual orientation is basically the social expression of one's own sexuality, then gender is basically a social expression of someone *else*'s sexuality. In the former case, one takes an object; in the latter case, one *is* an object. From the perspective of gender, then, we are all dumb blondes.

This need not be controversial. Feminists far less outrageous than Valerie have long argued that femininity expresses male sexuality pretty much from the beginning. The organizers of the famous Miss America protest in 1968—the origin of the famous bra-burning myth—railed in a press release against the "Degrading Mindless-Boob-Girlie Symbol" they considered the pageant to epitomize. None have put it more starkly than the anti-pornography feminist Catharine MacKinnon, whose 1989 book, *Toward a Feminist Theory of the State*, features a lengthy catalogue of examples:

> Each element of the female gender stereotype is revealed as, in fact, sexual. Vulnerability means the appearance/reality of easy sexual access; passivity means receptivity and disabled resistance, enforced by trained physical weakness;

softness means pregnability by something hard. Incompetence seeks help as vulnerability seeks shelter, inviting the embrace that becomes the invasion, trading exclusive access for protection ... from that same access. Domesticity nurtures the consequent progeny, proof of potency, and ideally waits at home dressed in Saran Wrap. Woman's infantilization evokes pedophilia; fixation on dismembered body parts (the breast man, the leg man) evokes fetishism; idolization of vapidity, necrophilia. Narcissism ensures that woman identifies with the image of herself man holds up: "Hold still, we are going to do your portrait, so that you can begin looking like it right away."

Indeed, MacKinnon has built an entire intellectual career out of the claim that "it is sexuality that determines gender, not the other way around." For her this means that men and women are constructed though an "eroticization of dominance and submission" whose central process is nonconsensual sexual objectification. Hence the famous line: "Man fucks woman; subject verb object."

To be female is to be an object—MacKinnon is right about this, I think. Where she errs is in the assumption that femaleness is a condition restricted to women. Gender is always a process of objectification: transgender women like Gigi Gorgeous know this probably better than most. Gender transition begins, after all, from the understanding that how you identify yourself subjectively—as precious and important as this identification may be—is nevertheless on its own basically worthless. If identity were all there were to gender, transition would be as easy as thinking it—a light bulb, suddenly switched on. Your gender identity would simply exist, in mute abstraction, and no one, least of all yourself, would care.

On the contrary, if there is any lesson of gender transition—from the simplest request regarding pronouns to the most invasive surgeries—it's that gender is something other people have to *give* you. Gender exists, if it is to exist at all, only in the structural generosity of strangers. When people today say that a given gender identity is "valid," this is true, but only tautologically so. At best it is a moral demand for possibility, but it does not, in itself, constitute the realization of this possibility. The truth is, you are not the central transit hub for meaning about yourself, and you probably don't even have a right to be. You do not get to consent to yourself, even if you might deserve the chance.

You do not get to consent to yourself—a definition of femaleness.

GINGER. Everybody knows that men
have much more respect for women
who're good at lapping up shit.

Once the drag queens leave, Bongi meets a girl who is
looking for a piece of shit. Her name is Virginia
Farnham, but she prefers to be called Ginger. "It so
aptly expresses me—brisk and spicy," she genially
explains. She is looking for a turd in a brown paper bag
that has gone missing. "Not to be nosey, but does this
turd have sentimental value?" Bongi asks, bemused.
"Don't be absurd," Ginger snaps. "It's for dinner."

Ginger is *Up Your Ass*'s resident Daddy's Girl. She
worships her psychoanalyst, a "leading exponent of
the doctrine that labor pains feel good." At Russell's
office, where she is the only woman on staff, she is flat-
tered by sexual harassment and loves to be thought of
as one of the boys. "I'm completely attuned to the
gripping dynamism of the male mind," she tells Bongi

breathlessly. "I talk to men on their level; I have virile, potent, sophisticated interests—I adore positions of intercourse, Keynesian economics, and I can look at dirty pictures for hours on end." She proudly parrots men's ideas; she is "flexible enough" to have "absorbed, not only Russell's, but Phil's and Bob's opinions with equal facility." She happily accepted being passed over for a promotion when her boss told her he'd be "lost without you." She loves male artists. She writes poetry—"pure feeling, uncluttered by a single thought, attitude or idea." As for the shit, Ginger just wants to serve it at the table to impress her guests.

In April 2016, comedian Jamie Loftus began taking videos of herself eating *Infinite Jest*, the thousand-page novel by David Foster Wallace, and uploading them to her Twitter account. In an interview with *Vice* about the project—a blend of performance art, physical comedy, and pure shitposting—Loftus explained that she'd gotten sick of being encouraged by self-important men at parties to give the famously opaque book a chance. "Basically [they] told me if I tried to read it and didn't like it, it was because I didn't understand it," she told the reporter. "I eat dog food on stage so I decided to do it as a joke and post it on Twitter after that." Over the next year or so, Loftus, who had been working at a bookstore, would film herself eating pages from the book. In the videos, she puts pages in sandwiches, chases them with beer, soaks them in coffee like biscotti. She mixes them into spaghetti; she stews them on the stove. When she's on the go, she chokes them down dry, mashing them into her face like a sweatshirt into a locker. She eats them at the mall, on the street, at her desk, in the club. She eats them at the Boston Gay Pride Parade. "I'm not gay," she tells the camera on her phone, "but I am eating a book, though."

Loftus told the *Vice* interviewer that she preferred to lube the pages first. "Only when I'm doing it onstage will I eat a page and swallow it and have that be totally dry," she explained. "But with the videos I'll usually create some sort of topping or moisten the page or it's just gonna be 10 miles of bad road for your body." The shift from reading to eating marked a sort of evolutionary relapse from vision to digestion: Loftus was, of course, stuffing the book in the wrong hole. What small percentage of print matter could be broken down by her intestinal system was being absorbed, uncomprehendingly, into her body; whatever remained was, of course, expelled as waste. A week or two into the project, Loftus called poison control to double check that eating *Infinite Jest* wouldn't kill her: "They were sort of like 'we can't sanction you doing this' but there's a way to do it. I couldn't be doing it too often, like I wanted to do a page a day but that's just not feasible to do that and stay alive."

At some point, Loftus made the decision to butt-chug *Infinite Jest*. From what I gather there used to be a video of the event, but like most of the project, it has disappeared. (In February 2018, Twitter suspended Loftus's account for making parody figure-skating videos in which skaters at the PyeongChang Winter Games appeared to perform to ironic subbed-in audio instead of music.) The *Vice* interview, thankfully, does include a picture of the act of anal ingestion. "I blended together five pages of *Infinite Jest* and a bunch of apples and made this thick sauce," Loftus reports. "Then I put it into a turkey baster that I bought and then I put a turkey baster into my asshole and did a handstand and had someone squeeze the turkey baster until it was empty." In the photo, Loftus is upside down, hands on the ground, feet in the air. She is wearing plain gray underwear and maybe a sports bra. Her friend is holding one of her ankles in one hand; with the other hand, she is holding the turkey baster. Loftus's right thigh is obscuring whether or not the baster is inserted. Her body looks like a doll's, or a mannequin's. Her face is completely out of the frame.

"Absorbing 'culture' is a desperate, frantic attempt to groove in an ungroovy world, to escape the horror of a sterile, mindless existence," declares the *SCUM Manifesto*, whose author never had anything but scorn for art made by men. "Lacking faith in their ability to change anything, resigned to the status quo, they *have* to see beauty in turds because, so far as they can see, turds are all they'll ever have." Loftus, a Daddy's Girl in her own right, isn't eating shit, exactly, but it sure *feels* like she is. The book is going up her ass, literally forced inside of her, in a kind of intellectual sodomy. Or rather, anti-intellectual: the project seems to have been as much a tremendous self-own as it was a critique of the cult of male genius. Loftus wasn't just performing female stupidity; she was also literally being a stupid female. She remarked to *Vice* that none of the men who tried to convince her to read *Infinite Jest* could give her a cohesive summary of what the book was actually like. Instead, they were like her: too dumb to know the difference. "I dunno," she told *Vice*. "It's a silly thing."

RUSSELL. You don't know what a female
is, you desexed monstrosity.

Appearances to the contrary, the word *female* is etymo-
logically unrelated to the word *male*. The latter comes,
through French, from *masculus*, the diminutive form
of the Latin word *mās*, also meaning "male," as said
of an animal. ("Further etymology unknown," states
the *Oxford English Dictionary* ominously.) The former,
albeit also through French, comes from the diminutive
form of Latin *fēmina*, "woman," an old participial
form meaning something like "she who suckles."
Through its Indo-European reconstruction, *female* is
distant cousins with over two dozen English words,
including *fecund*, *felicity*, *fennel*, *fetus*, *affiliate*, and
effete, as well as *fellatio*, from Latin *fellāre*, meaning
"to suck a dick."

As far back as the fourteenth century, the word *female*
was used to refer to women, with a particular emphasis

on their childbearing capacity, but it arguably did not acquire the technical sense of "a human mammal of the female sex" until the rise of the biological disciplines in the nineteenth century. In the United States, the man known as the father of gynecology, J. Marion Sims, built the field in the antebellum South, operating on enslaved women in his backyard, often without anesthesia—or, of course, consent. As C. Riley Snorton has recently documented, the distinction between biological females and women as a social category, far from a neutral scientific observation, developed precisely in order for the captive black woman to be recognized as female—making Sims's research applicable to his women patients in polite white society—without being granted the status of social and legal personhood. Sex was produced, in other words, precisely at the juncture where gender was denied. In this sense, a female has always been less than a person.

In the twentieth century, thanks to the research of French endocrinologist Alfred Jost, femaleness would come to be understood not just as a sex, but as the *default* sex of a mammalian fetus. Gynecologist Marci Bowers, a pioneer in the field of male-to-female gender surgeries, describes the vaginoplasty technique she has honed over years of practice by referring to precisely this principle of modern embryology. "As everyone has female genitalia early in gestation, the goal of the procedure is to reverse the current anatomy to its earlier configuration," her website explains. The idea here is that the human embryo, like that of most mammals, is originally female, becoming male only with the introduction of a masculinizing agent; hence, a vagina can be created from a penis by surgically rewinding the tape of early-stage sexual differentiation.

This developmental phenomenon effectively reverses the biblical creation myth in which Eve is created second, fashioned by God from Adam's rib—hence the term *Adam Principle*, introduced by controversial sexologist John Money in his book of the same name. Money's gloss on the Adam Principle is nothing short of bizarre:

If the Adam and Eve story had been written in a twentieth-century institute of embryological research, Eve would have been created first. Then, perhaps, an archangel would have descended with an injection needle laden with testosterone, the masculinizing hormone, and the combination of Eve plus testosterone would produce Adam. That short fable is no far-fetched product of an undisciplined imagination. It is a fable based on the scientific facts of modern embryology, which leaves no doubt whatsoever that in nature's order of things, it is Eve first, then Adam.

Obviously, Money's gotten the name wrong—by all rights, it should be the Eve Principle, given that in the fable Eve is, well, *principal*. But somehow Money manages to make the male sound even more impressive than before: a hormonal miracle, jacked up on heaven's performance-enhancing drugs. To prove the Adam Principle, Money offers up his research on androgen-insensitivity syndrome, a condition in which an individual is congenitally unresponsive to the solicitations of their Y chromosome and therefore looks, in the good doctor's words, "like a perfect female." Money has a hard time concealing his enthusiasm here:

> Without the competition of a male hormone, testicular estrogen does an excellent job of shaping a female. Her good looks may be so outstanding that they have enabled her, in some instances, to earn a living as a model. Such is the power of the Eve who lurks, forever imprisoned, in even the most full-bearded, bass-voiced, heroically androgenized and macho-minded of males!

Does he even know what he's saying?

MISS COLLINS. I face reality, and our
reality is that we're men.

Before I started testosterone blockers, I used to get very
angry—scary angry. I yelled a lot. In college, I bit my
arm a few times, hard, leaving delicate red marks in the
shape of my jaw. This may be essentialist, but it's also
true.

It was a lonely time, that fall I spent working on the
piano. I labored at night with the lights off, save for an
ugly fluorescent table lamp, scratching words no one
would ever read into an artwork no one would ever
care about. I knew this, even then, but I did it anyway,
because I had nothing else to do. I watched the tiny,
illegible words snaking their way across the soft pine.
More than once, the screwdriver I was using to etch the
keys would slip and abrade my palm. I was probably
depressed, but that language would never have occurred
to me then.

One of the many texts I transcribed alongside
SCUM was something called the *Manifesto of the
Futurist Woman*, a 1912 essay written by French artist
and dancer Valentine de Saint-Point in response to the
Italian Futurists. It's like if Valerie were a fascist (or
more of one). Saint-Point's on board with the Futurists'
glorification of the industrial machine, their lust for
violence, their unapologetic authoritarianism—she
just wants to make sure women get a piece of the
action. "Feminism is a political error," she scoffs. For
Saint-Point, the whole of humanity has up until
recently been mired in a feminine epoch of history:
sentimental, peaceful, anemic. What's needed is blood.
Men and women each, Saint-Point claims, can only be
whole by integrating both male and female elements,
and what's missing most right now, in both sexes, is
virility. It's a paradoxical conclusion: the only way for
women to fulfill themselves will be to undergo mascu-
linization. "Every woman must possess not only feminine virtues, but also masculine ones," Saint-Point
writes, "without which she is a female." The word here
in French is *femelle*, as said of livestock, not people.

I saw a lot of plays that semester, sometimes with
classmates, sometimes alone. I remember seeing *Mies
Julie* at St. Ann's Warehouse in Brooklyn, an adapta-
tion that transported Strindberg's forbidden love plot

from fin-de-siècle Sweden to postapartheid South Africa. Julie, now the daughter of a wealthy white Afrikaner, and John, a black servant on her father's estate, circle each other with vicious, electric eroticism. In the play's explosive climax, John grabs Julie and fucks her right there on the table. I remember the actor pulling down his pants, his naked ass to the audience, in the universal theatrical language of sex. It wasn't exactly a rape, but it wasn't not a rape, either. Afterwards, I marched down the street with some girls in my class, fuming. The staging had been gratuitous, I told them: lurid, exploitative, misogynistic. They let me rant. They had come to expect this kind of behavior from me. *Feminism*, they thought.

But sex was everywhere. I remember seeing *Einstein on the Beach* at the Brooklyn Academy of Music, Philip Glass's five-hour minimalist opera about Albert Einstein, in an extremely abstract sense of the word *about*. I went with the girl with whom I'd cheated on my ex. In the fourth act, there was a blackout, and after a moment, a long illuminated white bar appeared horizontal on the stage floor. Over an organ solo, the left side of the bar began to lift, like the hand of a clock, until the bar was perfectly vertical. When I watch videos of this scene on YouTube today, it takes about ten minutes; as I sat there in the dark, watching this great white erection, it felt like eternity. Valerie would have hated it.

When I got home that night, I probably watched porn. I did that most nights, guiltily hiding out in the shared bathroom, as if my roommates wouldn't notice: a sad, pretentious boy, furious about rape, hopelessly addicted to pornography. The two things fueled each other: the more righteous I felt in public, the more I could wallow, privately, in my shame. My anger made me angrier; what got me hot got hotter.

It would still be years before it would occur to me that I might be a woman. If the thought had presented itself then, I would have batted it away like an insect. I hated being a man, but I thought that was just how feminism felt. Being a man was my punishment for being a man. Anything else was greed.

BONGI. Why're *girls* called chicks?
After all, *men* have the peckers.

"Screwing is, for a man, a defense against his desire to be female," proclaims the *SCUM Manifesto*. The paradox of the male libido is that it isn't actually male. Nowhere is this more evident today than in the manosphere, that awfully named borough of the Internet where pickup artists, men's rights activists, incels, Men Going Their Own Way, and other alt-right communities go to commiserate, swap tips, and air their woman-hating and racism without fear of reprisal. At the heart of the manosphere lies the conviction that men—paradigmatically, though not always, white men—have lost status in the past fifty years, ultimately thanks to the rise of feminism. To awaken to this fact is to take the red pill—a phrase borrowed from the 1999 film *The Matrix*, whose hacker protagonist Neo is given the choice between a red pill and a blue. The latter will return Neo to his simulated everyday life with no memory of the choice; the former, which he picks, transports him out of the Matrix and into the real world where humanity has been enslaved by sentient machines. In recent years, the alt-right has co-opted the scene as a parable for seeing past feminist brainwashing to the truth: feminism is a disease, all women wish to be dominated, and nice guys finish last.

Of course, another interpretation of the red pill is possible. Trans women have claimed *The Matrix* as an allegory for gender transition since at least 2012, when director Lana Wachowski publicly came out as a trans woman while doing press for the film *Cloud Atlas*. (Her sister and codirector Lilly followed suit in 2016.) The symbolism is easy to find in the plot: Thomas Anderson's double life (he's a hacker by night), his chosen name (Neo), his vague but maddening sense that something is off about the world ("a splinter in your mind," resistance leader Morpheus calls it). Neo has dysphoria. The Matrix is the gender binary. You get it.

And then there's the red pill itself, less a metaphor for hormone therapy than a literal hormone. Many have pointed out online that back in the nineties, prescription estrogen was, in fact, red: the 0.625 mg Premarin tablet, derived in *Matrix*-like fashion from the urine of pregnant mares, came in smooth, chocolatey maroon. Trans allies on Twitter now gleefully brandish this fact as a *well, actually*–style rejoinder to the alt-right's recent co-optation of the red pill scene as a parable for "awakening" from feminist brainwashing.

There's something to this. Taken seriously, it suggests that the manosphere red-piller's resentment of immigrants, black people, and queers is a sadistic expression of his own gender dysphoria. In this reading, he is an abortive man, a beta trapped in an alpha's body, consumed with the desire to be female and desperately trying to repress it. His desire to increase his manhood is not primary, but a second-tier defense mechanism. Those around him assume he is a leader, a provider, a president; but his greatest fear is that they are mistaken. He radicalizes—shoots up a school, builds a wall—in order to avoid transitioning, the way some closeted trans women join the military in order to get the girl beaten out of them.

But there's another level. The Wachowski sisters, even if they knew about Premarin, could never have predicted that the most common form of prescription estrogen today would be blue. Aquamarine, actually— a tiny, coarse 2 mg estradiol pill supplied by Israeli pharmaceutical company Teva that turns to powder in your mouth. At present, I take the blue pill twice a day, once upon waking and once before bed, sending myself back into the simulation. By this logic, the hidden trans woman of *The Matrix* is not the messianic Neo, but Cypher, the sleazy traitor, who agrees to hand Morpheus over to the machines in exchange for being reinserted into the Matrix. "Ignorance is bliss," he tells the agents, mouth full of juicy, nonexistent steak. (Recall that *cipher* is an old word for zero.) "I don't wanna remember nothing. *Nothing*. You understand?"

Valerie would have approved of hormone therapy, I think. The *SCUM Manifesto* alludes, positively, to a futuristic world where men are transformed into women "by means of operations on the brain and nervous system." This was one of *SCUM*'s nongenocidal solutions for the few men who might remain after the revolution. Another, hinted at in a footnote, sounds a lot like the Matrix—a vast virtual reality network that men would willingly plug themselves into as "vicarious livers." "It will be electronically possible for [men] to tune into any specific female [they want] to and follow in detail her every movement," Valerie explains, declaring it a "marvelously kind and humane way" for women to treat their "unfortunate, handicapped fellow beings."

Isn't that the whole point of gender—letting someone else do your living for you?

BONGI. Come and get it.

When I visit the subreddit r/TheRedPill—one of the mano-sphere's more infamous ports of origin—I find that Reddit has quarantined it. "Are you sure you want to view this community?" the page asks me, telling me that the community is "dedicated to shocking or highly offensive content." I click through. I'm here to read a popular post from 2016 entitled "HOW TO GET LAID LIKE A WARLORD: 37 Rules of Approaching Model-Tier Girls." The post bills itself as a "complete guide to picking up 9s and 10s," though it hastens to add that it doesn't cover body language or "handling logistics." (I adjust my expectations.) Its author, who appears to be a man named Mike Haines, describes his past life as a sickly, shrimpy kid, frequently bullied by other, bigger boys. For most of his life, Mike has been involuntarily celibate, but after taking the red pill, he began regularly fucking 7s and 8s, and his current girlfriend is a 9 who's done some modeling work.

Mike's philosophical system is simple: Women are attracted to men, period. The only problem is that, for evolutionary reasons, they're also picky. Red-pillers describe this phenomenon as *hypergamy*: the tendency of women to seek increasingly attractive partners until their standards are impossibly high. Because they naturally prefer men with stronger frames— *frame* is a term of art in the pickup artist community, meaning something like "social comportment" or, if you like, "gender"—women unconsciously subject each potential suitor to a series of tests designed to put his frame under pressure: "Women want to submit to you. They want to submit to a strong man. But she can't submit to you if your frame is weaker than hers." Paradoxically, this means that male seduction is, in Mike's own words, a "passive process," not an active one. Mike clearly has little patience for cheap tricks or shortcuts: pickup lines, manipulation techniques, good looks or deep pockets. The name of the game is, simply, endurance. "Women have said things to me that are totally brutal—called me ugly, too short, a loser, etc.," Mike confides. "It doesn't penetrate."

And so transpires an unexpected reversal of roles: in order for a woman to be sure a man's worth submitting to, she must first dominate him. The man, conversely, must learn to look forward to his submission: "Women are wired in such a way that they can't become wet for a man unless he's overcome some kind of *resistance* to get her," Mike explains. "Hence, tests actually help you to seduce her. You want her to test you. The more tests you endure, the faster she'll sleep with you." The biggest loser—the one most open to abuse, suffering, humiliation—thus turns out to be the biggest winner. Desperate to prove he isn't a woman, he temporarily becomes one. A man will gladly "swim through a river of snot, wade nostril-deep through a mile of vomit, if he thinks there'll be a friendly pussy awaiting him," the *SCUM Manifesto* dryly observes.

You may think I'm being too generous to Mike and his fellow Red Pillers. Aren't these men entitled chauvinist pigs, wannabe rapists, domestic terrorists? Don't they value strength, force, assertiveness, independence? Sure. But if there is one thing the *SCUM Manifesto* teaches, it's that you must never assume that men actually want the things they *say* they want. "The male has one glaring area of superiority over the female," the manifesto asserts: "public relations." For Valerie, the single greatest hoax in the history of human civilization was the simple idea that men are men. The patriarchal system of sexual oppression therefore existed not to express man's maleness, but to conceal his femaleness. "He hates his passivity, so he projects it onto women, defines the male as active, then sets out to prove that he is," writes Valerie. She had already dramatized this phenomenon in *Up Your Ass*, where Bongi goads Russell, a Red Piller *avant la lettre*, into fucking her behind a bush, just to show she can. Russell is initially repulsed, but he can't help himself. "I could never make love to you, but I *am* louse enough to screw you," he snarls, lunging at her. But Bongi stops him. "First get on your knees and say: 'Please can I do it to you?'" she commands. He obeys. "You're a good doggie," she smirks.

Indeed, this is the surprising core of the whole Red Pill theory of seduction: never stop begging for it. Mike concedes that being forced to undergo a battery of tests just to get some ass "might seem 'unfair' to you." But he doesn't care. "If you can't handle the abuse from some blonde chick in a bar," writes Haines, "how the fuck are you going to handle beating a 7ft tall man to death with your bare hands when he and his tribe invade your village and try to gang-rape your girl?" The star of this primitivist metaphor is, interestingly, the very warlord whose ability to get laid the post promises to impart to readers. Only here, he isn't them—he's their invisible competition, whose animalistic powers of abuse have been entrusted to the woman they see before them. "Women will test you brutally when they want to sleep with you," Mike cautions. This reminds him of the film *Fight Club*, because of course it does:

> Getting a hot woman into bed is like the hazing scene in *Fight Club* where the new recruits are lined up outside the door. Tyler berates the recruits with personal insults. "Too old, go away." "Too fat, go away." He forces them to stand outside for days. He tells them there's no possibility they're getting in. Most give up. But the few who stay are ultimately invited inside. Seducing the hottest women is the same. It's a WAR OF ATTRITION.

Like *The Matrix*, *Fight Club* is a popular point of reference in the manosphere. The film is easily described in alt-right terms: a milquetoast beta meets a rebellious alpha named Tyler Durden, and together the two found a men's fighting ring; when the club starts committing acts of terrorism, the beta discovers that Tyler is an alter ego he has unconsciously created for himself in order to escape his meaningless middle-class life. It is therefore all the stranger that in Mike's analogy, the role of Tyler Durden is given to the hot girl. The girl is the hazer, screaming at recruits like a drill sergeant, beating them with a broom, while her seducer assumes the position of the schlubby would-be initiate whom Tyler dismisses with disgust: "You're too old, fat man. Your tits are too big. Get the fuck off my porch." Men are not men. Men are never men.

In 2018, when the *Guardian* asked *Fight Club* author Chuck Palahniuk what he thought of the film's popularity on the far right, he replied that the phenomenon reflected "how few options men have in terms of metaphors" for their experience of gender. Asked what he thought would come of the alt-right, he answered that he thought it was too fringe to last. "It might be comparable to Valerie Solanas's Society for Cutting Up Men," he told the interviewer. "The extreme always goes away."

BONGI. I star in movies for stag parties.
But I've got professional integrity—I
only work for the top directors.

The manosphere is deeply divided over the issue of pornography. For many in the alt-right, pornography—and the addiction to masturbation with which it corresponds—is genuinely dangerous for men. The far-right fraternal group Proud Boys, who made headlines in 2018 for beating up antifa protestors on the Upper East Side, requires that all second-tier members subscribe to what they call NoWanks, giving up masturbation and pornography for thirty days at a time. (At the end of a cycle, Proud Boys are given the option of a single cheat wank.) In a 2015 video for the right-wing website The Rebel, Proud Boys founder Gavin McInnes explains that, by providing young men with a fleeting but addictive hypermasculine delirium, pornography has made it impossible for them to date, marry or reproduce effectively: "You've fooled your brain into thinking you're inseminating 10s, and then when you're with a real woman, your brain goes, "What are you doing with one broad? She's not even a 10, she's like a 7. Why are you wasting my time with this?'" While he admits that being antiporn sounds like "an Andrea Dworkin thing," McInnes assures viewers that it's worth their time. "I'll be whistling on my bike, I sing in the shower," he tells the camera through his hipster beard. "I really feel more alive."

Pornography is what it feels like when you think you have an object, but really the object has *you*. It is therefore a quintessential expression of femaleness. Of course, anxieties over porn addiction are hardly exclusive to the manosphere, especially now that digital technologies, especially smartphones, seem to have placed an infinitude of free, easily accessible pornographic material beneath the nation's vulnerable thumbs. Hence what is known as Rule 34 of the Internet: If it exists, there is porn of it. This has left the social field well lubricated for periodic moral panics about the sexual degeneracy presumed to prowl the public playgrounds of the digital. The decades-long cancer of go-go bars and porn theaters in Times Square may have finally been cut out by the family-friendly scalpel of the Walt Disney Company, but *Lion*

King–themed erotic cartoons can now be accessed by any twelve-year-old with Internet access and a clue.

Feminists, meanwhile, have been debating pornography for decades, since it became a centerpiece of the so-called sex wars of the eighties. For activists like Catharine MacKinnon and Andrea Dworkin, pornography, with its graphic depictions of female degradation, was the patriarchal institution par excellence, the key to understanding all sex between men and women. Others, sometimes grouped under the label "pro-sex," wondered how their feminist commitments might be reconciled with genuinely pleasurable experiences of dominance and submission—not to mention, eroticism generally. Tensions between the two camps boiled over at the famous "Pleasure and Danger" conference held at Barnard College in 1982. A week before the conference, antipornography feminists phoned Barnard officials to warn them of the conference's antifeminist agenda; those administrators responded by confiscating 1,500 copies of the elaborate, sometimes graphic seventy-two-page program organizers had lovingly prepared. The day of the conference, while participants gave and heard papers on the theme of "pleasure and danger" in female sexuality, members of the radical feminist group Women Against Pornography passed out leaflets vilifying the conference and accusing women by name of collaboration with the patriarchy. At stake in all this was the question that Amber Hollibaugh raised at Barnard: "Is there 'feminist' sex? Should there be?" Or to put it bluntly: can women have sex without getting fucked?

Valerie's answer is still the best one: No, but who cares? "Sex is the refuge of the mindless," she gripes in the *SCUM Manifesto*, which isn't against sex so much as deeply unimpressed by it. "Sex is not part of a relationship," Valerie writes. "On the contrary, it is a solitary experience, non-creative, a gross waste of time." She had it, of course—sometimes with men, sometimes with women, sometimes for money—and she certainly had no time for the cheap, quasi-religious moralism that antiporn feminists would cultivate in the years to come. If anything, she was an accelerationist about the whole thing: "SCUM gets around . . . and around and around . . . they've seen the whole show—every bit of it—the fucking scene, the dyke scene, they've covered the whole waterfront, been under every dock and pier—the peter pier, the pussy pier . . . you've got to go through a lot of sex to get to anti-sex." Ti-Grace Atkinson reports finding a piece of erotica that Valerie had written for *Hustler* magazine among the latter's belongings in 1968. "Typical male pornography, S&M, really written from that place," she told Fahs. "I assume she was writing it to make some money and you can't play around too much if you want the money."

ALVIN. I guess it's just the romantic in me.

Bongi flags down a nicely dressed man with the intention of hustling him into buying her dinner. (Valerie did this kind of thing all the time.) His name is Alvin, and he fancies himself a ladies' man. He reads all the "more zestful men's magazines— *Tee-Hee*, *Giggle*, *Titter*, *Lust*, *Drool*, *Slobber*, and, just for thoroughness, *Lech*." His apartment is arranged around an enormous revolving bed he read about in *Playboy*. "Why'd you approach me?" he asks Bongi, fishing. "You must have sensed something unusual." She gives a practiced pout. "*Sensed* it! I was over*whelmed* by it," Bongi exclaims. "Any woman can see you're a ball of fire." She ushers him to a nearby expensive restaurant; she'll end up giving him a brisk hand job in the alley for twenty-five bucks. He scurries away, disappointed not to have been given a chance to perform.

In 2013, onetime child actor Joseph Gordon-Levitt wrote and directed a romantic comedy called *Don Jon*. In the film, Gordon-Levitt stars at Jon Martello, a latter-day Don Juan from a working-class Italian-American family in New Jersey. Jon's reputation for being able to bed any woman he pleases has earned him the nickname "Don Jon" among his friends. But Jon has a secret: he's addicted to online pornography. The film depicts his addiction through a series of quick, graphic cuts: the chirpy fanfare of a booting-up laptop, the unassuming triangular play button of a pornographic video, a close-up on Jon's face, a climactic musical cue, a hand pulling a tissue from a box and then the same tissue, now crumpled, tossed into a wastebasket to the sound of a digital file's being deleted. This masturbatory loop is mirrored, during the day, by Jon's unbroken Sunday routine: Jon fastidiously making his bed, Jon cursing at other drivers, Jon running up the steps to church, Jon's face behind the confessional window, Jon swaggering to the weight room at the gym, Jon pumping iron to the rhythm of a Hail Mary, Jon eating dinner in a wifebeater at his parents' house while his macho father yells at a televised football game. The message is clear: Jon's in a rut.

Jon's addictive behavior ends up sabotaging his budding relationship with a beautiful girl named

Barbara (Scarlett Johansson, obviously), who finally puts out after he starts taking a night-school class in order to escape his current employment in the service industry. When Barbara nearly catches him sneaking out of bed to watch porn, Jon puffs out his chest and tells her that only "fucking losers watch porn." He's talking about himself, of course. Whereas being on top means he's expected to "do all the work" in sex with women, pornography does all his desiring for him. "I don't gotta say anything, I don't gotta do anything," he explains in voiceover, "I just fucking *lose* myself." Jon's eyes slide in and out of focus, his mouth hangs slightly ajar, his skin dimly electric with the guilty glow of the screen. Like all men, Jon watches porn not to have power, but to give it up.

In short, pornography feminizes him. This is where the film's implicit theory of pornography—call it anti-porn postfeminism—both joins and splits with those of its forerunners in the sex wars. *Don Jon* basically agrees with the MacKinnonite doctrine that porn is structured by the eroticization of dominance and submission—but it locates this power dynamic not in the sex acted out between the commanding men and degraded women onscreen, but in the sex unfolding between the addictive pornographic image and the essentially female viewer it dominates. When Barbara discovers that Jon's browser history is stuffed full of porn sites, she will accuse Jon of having "more sex with that thing"—his screen—than with his own girl-friend. When she leaves him, he relapses hard, barely leaving his apartment for days.

Luckily, Jon finds help, in the form of an emotion-ally fulfilling relationship with a wise older woman named Esther whom he meets at night school (Julianne Moore, obviously). After making slow, tender love to Esther on her couch, Jon mans up: he stops sleeping around, starts singing in traffic, mixes up his routine, stands up to his domineering father, and never watches porn again. In *Don Jon*'s concluding montage, Jon and Esther stare into each other's eyes while Jon's voiceover describes their new, "two-way" kind of love. "I do lose myself in her," he confides, "I can tell she's losing herself in me, and we're just fucking lost together." The film closes with Jon and Esther making gorgeously sunlit love in Jon's bed, each penetrating the other's eyes with their own in an accelerating series of radiant shot–reverse shots. Neither of them, we are asked to believe, are female.

BONGI. Downright perverse.

Almost every night, for at least a year before I transitioned, I would wait till my girlfriend had fallen asleep and slip out of bed for the bathroom with my phone. I was going on Tumblr to look at something called sissy porn. I'd discovered it by accident one night, scrolling lazily down a pornographic rabbit hole. At first, I'd been into JOI videos—the acronym stands for "jerk-off instruction." In a typical JOI, a solo female performer directs presumptively male viewers to masturbate, in detail. The whole thing is unusually meta, even for porn: many JOI actresses will explicitly shame viewers for wasting their time masturbating instead of fucking a real woman like herself. Humiliation is therefore a frequent theme. Orgasms are often ruined or withheld entirely; affectations of disgust or amusement at the thought of the viewer's tiny penis are common.

But these videos pale in comparison to sissy porn. In the right corner of Reddit, you can find a whole genre of posts concerned that sissy porn has irreversibly altered the course of their lives. "Did sissy porn make me trans or was I trans all along?" a worried user asks in a post from 2014:

> About 3 years ago, I discovered sissy hypno videos, which in a nutshell are flashing subjective images telling you to wear panties, be girly, suck cock, and even take hormones. I became completely obsessed with these videos. Nothing got me off like these. It got to the point where I started wearing panties and imagining myself as a girl when I would masturbate.

The poster, currently living as a gay man, is "95% percent sure" that she is a closeted transgender woman, noting her preference for female playmates as a child and extreme postpubescent social anxiety, her failure to become aroused during sex with men (no matter how studly), and her sometimes suicidal depression at the thought of continuing to live as a man. But the fear expressed by the title—namely, that the poster's obsession with sissy porn has made her want to become a woman—hangs over the whole post.

Posts like this one describe feelings of shame, anxiety, confusion, and alarm. They fear that real trans women just aren't into this kind of thing. One user writes that despite her never having felt male and her hatred for erections, when she told her therapist that she was addicted to sissy erotica, her therapist told her she just had a kink. "Real MTFs don't do that," said her therapist. "Ever."

In fact, transsexuality has a long history of being considered a paraphilia. Since the eighties, sexologist Ray Blanchard has defended the classification of transsexual women into two distinct erotic types. Trans people and their advocates have largely rejected this typology, not least because Blanchard—a truly loathsome man who on his own justifies the inclusion of "psychiatrists and clinical psychologists" on SCUM's hit list—considers trans women to be male. "All gender dysphoric males who are not sexually oriented toward men are instead sexually oriented toward the thought or image of themselves as women," he proposed in a 1989 paper. He named the latter tendency *autogynephilia*, coined to sound like the Greek for "love of oneself as a woman." With this concept, Blanchard seems to have been interested in shifting sex researchers' focus from the transvestite's fetish objects—for instance, "the physical properties of clothing used for cross-dressing (silky textures, striking colors)"—towards a more fundamental erotic investment in the idea of the self as female.

Never uncontroversial in sexology circles, Blanchard's work was introduced to a broader audience in 2003 by *The Man Who Would Be Queen*, a lurid little volume that billed itself as a popular book about unpopular truths. The book's author, psychologist J. Michael Bailey, leans heavily on the theory of autogynephilia, which he presents as settled scientific fact. The theory has thus become a touchstone for trans-hating feminists looking to cast trans women as male perverts. "The term transgender was coined . . . to create a more acceptable face for a practice previously understood as a 'paraphilia'—a form of sexual fetishism," writes noted transphobe Sheila Jeffreys in a book that cites Blanchard's work liberally. Jeffreys also happens to discuss sissy porn at length. "The use of the term 'sissy' is illuminating since it is very clearly a term of abuse based upon women's subordinate status," she claims, disgusted. "There is no positive association with women attached to this practice, only a degrading and demeaning one."

What Blanchard hoped to describe with the term *autogynephilia* was, of course, exactly what the *SCUM Manifesto* had described twenty years earlier as the psychological disease shared by *all men*. Indeed, if everyone is female—and I'm hoping you're starting to believe that they are—then autogynephilia describes not an obscure paraphilic affliction but rather *the basic structure of all human sexuality*. This is not just because everyone has an erotic image of themselves as female—they do—but the assimilation of any erotic image is, by nature, female. To be female is, in every case, to become what someone else wants. At bottom, everyone is a sissy.

ARTHUR. Fuck is in the air; it's overpowering; it carries you away with it, sucks you right up.

If you've ever seen sissy porn, you'll know that turning people female is exactly what sissy porn says it does. Also known as forced feminization or "forced fem," sissy porn seems to have begun circulating principally on the microblogging platform Tumblr in or around 2013. The genre is characteristically user-generated rather than produced by a traditional studio: in large part, sissy content creators would appropriate videos, stills, and animated GIFs from mainstream heterosexual or "shemale" pornography—intellectual property is notoriously difficult to protect in today's porn industry—and modify this material with captions altering their original meaning. In late 2018, when the microblogging platform moved to ban graphic sexual content, sissy porn creators, like many other sex workers, were forced to flee to other platforms, including Twitter and Instagram.

Sissy porn's central conceit is that the women it depicts (some cis, some trans, mostly but not always white) are in fact former men who have been feminized ("sissified") by being forced to wear makeup, wear lingerie, and perform acts of sexual submission. This is executed through the unique form of second-person address in which captions are typically written: sissy porn directly addresses its viewers and presumes to inform them of their own desires: "You love to be fucked in the ass," for instance, or "You want to suck cock." (Sissy porn often uses *cock* as an uncountable mass noun, like *water* or *sugar*, presumably because there can always be more.) Captions further instruct viewers to understand that the very act of looking at sissy porn itself constitutes an act of sexual degradation, with the implication that, whether they like it or not, viewers will inevitably be transformed into females themselves. This makes sissy porn a kind of meta-pornography, that is, porn about what happens to you when you watch porn. In other words, sissy porn takes the implicitly feminizing effect of all pornography (even the most vanilla) and promotes it to the level of explicit content—often with spectacular results.

At the center of sissy porn lies the asshole, a kind of universal vagina through which femaleness can always be accessed. In the midst of the AIDS crisis, the gay male critic Leo Bersani famously wrote that public horror of anal sex betrayed a hateful envy of the "intolerable image of a grown man, legs high in the air, unable to refuse the suicidal ecstasy of being a woman." Sissy porn takes this literally. Getting fucked makes you female because fucked is what a female is. At the same time, sissy porn remains wholly uninterested in who's doing the fucking. Men appear, when they appear, only in fragments: a hand, an ass, a stray leg. Tops are props; their function is purely structural. "To call a man an animal is to flatter him," Valerie writes in *SCUM*. "He's a machine, a walking dildo. It's often said that men use women. Use them for what? Surely not pleasure."

Sissy porn makes frequent use of fetish objects—makeup, lingerie, breasts, high heels, and the color pink—but unlike the classical Freudian fetish, these objects *promise* castration, instead of warding against it. For Freud, the fetish was a clear substitute for the "absent female phallus." The little boy, traumatized by the discovery that his mother has no penis and fearing lest the same fate befall his own, looks for reassurance to an object that can replace that penis—a high-heeled shoe, for instance, or the touch of velvet. The fetish is thus "a token of triumph over the threat of castration and a protection against it." Yet even Freud knew that the fetish, in disavowing castration, thereby implicitly acknowledged it; sissy porn exploits this weakness, transforming the fetish from an assurance that the penis will be kept safe into a guarantee that the penis will be lost forever. This means that, in cases where the sissy is a trans woman, even her own fetishized penis becomes a symbol of castration. If her penis is limp, it is mocked for its tiny size and called a "clitty"; if it is hard, this is simply proof that she is enjoying her degradation.

In fact, to be a sissy is always to lose your mind. The technical term for this is *bimboification*. Captions often instruct viewers to submit themselves to hypnosis, brainwashing, brain-melting, dumbing down, and other techniques for scooping out intelligence. "Why do I like the concept of being a Bimbo?" asks one user. "It's because my brain is always full. I'm always worrying if Master truly loves me. Am I enough? Am I making good choices? Do people actually like me? How can I live in a country like this with this current political climate? Where else could I even imagine going?" The gestures most often looped in GIF format almost always register the evacuation of will: wilting faces, trembling legs, eyes rolled back into heads. Even the GIF format itself communicates this, a kind of centrifuge for distilling the femaleness to its barest essentials—an open mouth, an expectant asshole, blank, blank eyes.

Sissy porn did make me trans. At very least it served as a neat allegory for my desire to be female—and increasingly, I thought, for all desire as such. Too often, feminists have imagined powerlessness as the suppression of desire by some external force, and they've forgotten that more often than not, desire *is* this external force. Most desire is nonconsensual; most desires aren't desired. Wanting to be a woman was something that descended upon me, like a tongue of fire, or an infection—or a mental illness, at least if you believe the *Diagnostic and Statistical Manual of Mental Disorders*, where gender dysphoria can be found sandwiched between frigidity and pyromania. The implication is obvious: No one in their right mind would want to be female.

Which, remember, is all of us.

BONGI. Let the guys ram each other in
the ass and leave the women alone.

As she catcalls women on the street, Bongi is joined by
two pickup artists. The stage directions identify them
as "two cats, one white and one spade." *Spade* here
means "black," a slang term dating back to the Harlem
Renaissance; coming from a white girl like Valerie, it
sounds like a slur. The men hit on Bongi, who rebuffs
them, before turning their attention to the same
women she's been bothering. The white one makes a
polite, ineffectual pass at a flashy girl walking by.
"Beat it, Little Boy," she spits. His friend thinks he can
do better. "Step aside and let a man operate," he
boasts.

SPADE CAT. Good evening, Goddess. Forgive what
may sound like mere hyperbole, but to me you
are a goddess.

CHICK. I can well understand your reaction; you've captured the inner me. Is that Boy Scout over there a friend of yours?

SPADE CAT. A mere acquaintance, but enough of an acquaintance for me to know he's not at all the man for you; his technique's as washed-out as his skin.

CHICK. And yours's as intense as yours?

SPADE CAT. You're perceptive.

The caricature is so obvious that the chick reads it as quickly as the reader. She's also, well, into it. As she and the spade cat retire to his place to get better acquainted, the white cat shuffles off, grumbling in dejection. "I may as well turn in my yo-yo; all the swinging chicks're either queer or they go with spades," he pouts. "A white man doesn't stand a chance nowadays." In a clever director's hands, the scene might be an effective satire of what we could call a right-wing fantasy of national cuckoldry: the emasculated white man, spit-roasted by black men at one end and lesbians at the other, resigns himself to a life of sexual frustration. An incel is born.

On August 12, 2017, a group of neo-Nazis, Klan members, and alt-righters held a violent rally in Charlottesville, Virginia, that resulted in the murder of antifascist protestor Heather Heyer. Three days later, the prolific sissy porn creator known as Sissy Mindy—who has frequently posted topical content—posted an image to her Tumblr featuring a white woman performing oral sex on a black man. Her head is fully sideways, her eyes wide, as if surprised by its girth. "Fight against intolerance and racism," reads the overlaid caption. "Suck big black cock." The trope of the black man's penis as large, threatening, and tremendously potent is an old one, of course, the standby excuse for lynchings and white supremacist terror, and it's found all across the pornographic spectrum, where it's known as BBC—from glossy mainstream series like *Blacked*, in which nubile white girls lose their interracial virginity, to one of sissy porn's closer relatives, cuckolding porn, in which white boyfriends and husbands are forced to watch, and occasionally participate, as black men fuck their eager wives and girlfriends.

The classic explanation for this fetish is the revolutionary Frantz Fanon's theory of negrophobia as a kind of murderous envy: the white man, projecting onto the black man the "infinite virility" he worries he lacks, proceeds to revenge himself against the latter, prototypically in the form of lynching. What sissy porn's use of the trope suggests, however, is that when Fanon supposed that the negrophobe might be a repressed homosexual, he was only half-right. The paradox of white supremacy, of course, is that it's actually an inferiority complex: the white man, who could have just as easily fantasized that the black man's penis was smaller than his own—it would be fantasy either way, after all—nevertheless opts to imagine himself as a sexual failure, going limp in the presence of the black man's unlimited sexual potency.

In other words, the true threat, which in Sissy Mindy's post becomes an alluring promise, is not that the black man will prevent the white racist from being a man, but that the black man will remind the white man that he never wanted to be a man in the first place. Sissy Mindy registers this anxiety with the hashtags she places on the post, which include "BBC slave," "black supremacy," and "white genocide." The last of these is a decades-old conspiracy theory about government-run white extinction programs (immigration, low fertility rates, abortion, etc.) that's recently found new life as a popular alt-right talking point on social media. In this form, sissy porn becomes, as it were, the truest version of itself: a parodic expression of the alt-right's most repressed sexual fantasies. The cheeky implication appears to be not only that becoming female is a bit like dying, but also that white sissification might constitute a form of erotic reparations for the devastation wrought by chattel slavery.

That's a joke, of course, whether or not you find it funny. No one actually expects one blow job to change anything. In a sense, that's the point: females and politics never mix. After decades of tedious feminist debates over agency, one thing is clear: women may be capable of political action, but females never are. Ultimately, the phrase *forced feminization* is redundant: the female is always the product of force, and force is invariably feminizing. This is why environments designed to forcibly masculinize their inhabitants—college fraternities and the US military come to mind—inevitably end up expressing their central contradiction (anyone *forced* to be a man couldn't possibly *be* a man) not just through rape and sexual assault (of both men and women by men), but also with a set of hazing rituals in which men are forced to undergo feminizing sex acts. It's also why the same contingent of feminists who seek to unmask trans women as male pretenders may almost always be relied upon to cast sex workers as the feminized victims of human traffickers—there is too much female among each group and not enough woman. If sex workers were really women, they would rescue themselves from the sexual objectification that makes them women; if trans women were women, they would have the good sense not to be.

GINGER. Let your soul sway gently in the void.

When I finally debuted the piano project at the end of the term, I delivered a manifesto I had prepared to accompany it. I wrote it very quickly, in two or three nights, deep into the dark morning. I still have it on my computer, tucked with embarrassment into some dusty folder, like a letter from an ex. The thing is called "Apocalypse Manifesto: Towards a Radioactive Art." It's intentionally messy: a thicket of mismatched fonts, upside-down text, collaged black-and-white images. Grand statements about artistic practice are punctuated by weird sexual outbursts. ("Oh god dick give it to me baby," I write, a baffling reference to Fluxus artist Dick Higgins.) Andy Warhol makes two appearances, or at least his work does: first, a Marilyn Monroe silkscreen, turned on its side and covered in text, with the words MASS CULTURE above it (I know); then, the album art for *The Velvet Underground & Nico*, duplicated severally, each banana sloppily pasted over the next—another clever dick joke, I must have thought. I was obsessed with Allan Kaprow's 1986 essay "Art Which Can't Be Art." I reproduced a big chunk of it in my manifesto:

> I decided to pay attention to brushing my teeth, to watch my elbow moving. I would be alone in my bathroom, without art spectators. There would be no gallery, no critic to judge, no publicity. This was the crucial shift that removed the performance of everyday life from all but the memory of art. I could, of course, have said to myself, "Now I'm making art!!" But in actual practice, I didn't think much about it.

Sentiments like these soothed me. I was stridently anti-institution in those days. "There are no museums which are not history museums," I crack in a footnote. In the final pages, I point out that every manifesto *is* an apocalypse, in the original sense of both words: revelation. True art, I thought, would become coterminous with life itself. True art would be nothing at all.

As I was writing this book, I was invited to give a talk at a film festival in the Midwest. Not a "talk," exactly—the programmer who spoke to me referred to it as a Provocation, a brief, challenging performance intended to force the audience into wrestling with a difficult or strange idea. Casting about for an idea, I began to imagine something akin to *Cut Piece*, which artist Yoko Ono famously performed at Carnegie Hall in 1965, not far from the hotel in Chelsea where Valerie was then putting the finishing touches on *Up Your Ass*. You can find videos of *Cut Piece* on YouTube. During the performance, Ono sits onstage with her legs tucked under her, wearing a long-sleeved black blouse and a black skirt. Her hair is in a short, clean bun; her face is impassive. On the floor next to her, there are some long silver scissors. You can hear audience members moving around, chatting, giggling. One by one, participants male and female approach her and cut into her clothing with the long silver scissors that sit beside her. Some are modest, others forceful, still others amused. About seven minutes in, her blouse is gone, and a young man in a puffy white shift gleefully appoints himself the one who will cut off her camisole, and then her bra. When he cuts her bra straps, she holds the cups in place with crossed hands. Ono breaks character briefly here to roll her eyes at him. The audience laughs, because it's funny, and it's also horrifying. The term "death drive" is too strong to describe what's going on in *Cut Piece*; it's more of a death drift, limp and aimless. Yoko isn't doing anything, after all; that's the whole point. She's being done to. She hasn't given her consent so much as given up consenting.

I performed six times at the film festival, each time before a documentary about an evasive stage magician. I began by announcing that I had in my hand a small remote control, and I needed a volunteer to hold on to it for me. The remote had a button with an arrow on it, and I invited the volunteer to press that button as many times as she liked for the remainder of the performance. (Five times out of six, the volunteer was a woman.) I explained that I was a writer who tended to write about gender and sexuality, and that I also had recently purchased a new vagina—by which I meant, I had paid a plastic surgeon to rearrange my old bits into some new bits. "So I got to thinking," I would say, letting my gaze wander toward the ceiling. "What if I came out onstage with a vibrator inserted into my vagina, and what if I solicited a volunteer and gave them a remote control, and what if that remote control had a button on it which, when pressed, turned the vibrator on, and what if I gave my consent, in front of everyone, for the volunteer to press that button as many times as they liked for the duration of the performance, and just let everyone watch?"

By this point, the audience was laughing—as much, I hoped, from suspicion and scandal as humor. I told them about *Cut Piece* and why I admired it. I told them, as a friend of a friend had suggested to me, that we might call my hypothetical performance *Cunt Piece*. I suggested to the audience that this would be a private show, between me and one other person. "The rest of you wouldn't actually be watching the performance, you'd be watching yourself *fail* to watch it," I told them. "Maybe you'd be listening to see if you could hear the vibrator, maybe you'd be watching my face to see if I betrayed any signs that the vibrator was on, but at the end of the day you probably wouldn't be able to see the volunteer, to see if she was actually pressing the button, and even if you could see, you wouldn't be able to tell if the remote was working, and even if it was working, you simply couldn't be sure whether I actually did have a vibrator inside me, or whether I even had a vagina at all, or whether I had just made the whole thing up just to fuck with you."

And that was it. For the most part, I was telling the truth. I had, in fact, recently undergone vaginoplasty. I did, in fact, have a vibrator on my person, but it was a small clitoral vibrator, not an insertable one, and it didn't have the size or power to genuinely arouse me. I would have liked it to, actually: it would have created more risk on my part, instead of the mere illusion of risk. But I could, in fact, feel it every time the volunteer pressed the button on the remote, which most of them did—even after learning that by doing so they might have been having sex with me at a distance. A few even seemed to become emboldened by this possibility, pressing the button over and over with gusto.

At no point did I mention Valerie. The performance was too brief to describe my attraction to her, my obsession with her work. It was exactly the kind of sexual stunt that Valerie both loved and loved to hate: unreadable, vaguely hostile, but also weirdly passive, right at the nexus of SCUM and Daddy's Girl, where most women, including Valerie, lived. Perhaps I also felt possessive. It was a private show after all, but its audience of one had died thirty years before, probably from emphysema, kneeling on the floor of her room at the Bristol Hotel in San Francisco. Praying, I suppose, to no one.

ARTHUR. I *am* terrible, aren't I?

In the summer of 1967, Valerie was frequenting the Factory, trying to cajole Andy Warhol into directing and producing *Up Your Ass*. One day, she interviewed him, and he recorded it. On the tape, Andy asks Valerie if she works for the CIA. Valerie asks Andy how he gets off. Other parts play as if she is interviewing him to lead the men's auxiliary of SCUM.

VALERIE. What effect has SCUM had on your life?
ANDY. Uh, it makes me like girls more.
VALERIE. Why? . . .
ANDY. Before they were only boys.
VALERIE. Now they're what?
ANDY. Girls . . . That girls didn't exist before.
VALERIE. You thought there were only boys.
ANDY. Yeah.
VALERIE. That there was only one sex.

ANDY. That's right.

VALERIE. And now you know there are two.

ANDY. Now there are two . . .

It's disorienting for me to read this now. Andy is my birth name. It's alien to me now, like an old photograph, or a leg that's fallen asleep. A few people still use it, but this is my fault. When I first came out, I told people I would be going by Andi. When spoken aloud, the living name was identical with the dead one.

At the end of *Up Your Ass*, Bongi meets a woman named Arthur. "That's not *my* name; it's my *hus*band's," she explains. It's not clear whether Bongi wants to fight her or fuck her; before long, the two are shooting the shit. They discuss the tedium of Arthur's marriage, her husband's insatiable sex drive. For a bit, they are interrupted by Arthur's son, a whiny boy of five or six who has, in an attempt to give himself an erection, gummed up his pee-hole with glue. Arthur waves him off with contempt. She hates her life. She's seen the same shrink as Ginger, the turd-eating Daddy's Girl, but it hasn't made a difference. "I've tried relating to the emptiness," she confides, "but it doesn't work— he doesn't relate back." In an unexpected reversal, Arthur propositions Bongi. "I bet you'd be a crazy lover," Arthur flirts. "Actually, I'm a lousy lover," Bongi admits. "I'm too good a talker." It's true; she is. As much as Bongi spends *Up Your Ass* talking about being a woman of action, it's mostly just that: talk. It's Arthur, the woman with her husband's name, who ends up doing something. Her son comes back, crying and asking her to keep him company. She strangles him instead, burying him on the street. Murder concealed, Arthur joins Bongi in harassing a passing broad, "a beautiful, low-down, funky doll"—just Valerie's type. The play ends.

Andy Warhol shot Valerie Solanas in 1967, paying her twenty-five dollars to take part in his film *I, a Man*. In part, the gig was Warhol's way of apologizing for losing the copy of *Up Your Ass* that Valerie had given him. "She came right over and we filmed her in a short scene on a staircase," Andy recalled. "She was actually funny and that was that." In the film, Valerie's wearing the hat she always has on in the pictures of her I've seen; I had assumed her hair was short, but in fact she has a messy ponytail. Her voice is bouncy and natural, with a strong New Jersey accent. She's rebuffing the advances of a man whose ass she had grabbed in the elevator. "I'm a sucker for squishy ass," she admits, "but what else have you got?" When he persists, she finally tells him the truth. "Your instincts tell you to chase chicks, right?" she asks, a few steps above him on the stairs, gesturing with her cigarette. "Right!" he answers. "My instincts tell me to do the same thing." Watching this, I realize that I find Valerie extremely attractive, which probably means she never would have agreed to sleep with me.

Valerie Solanas shot Andy Warhol on June 3, 1968. The bullet damaged his stomach, liver, throat, both his lungs, and his spleen, which the doctors would remove during emergency surgery. When he reached the hospital, he was pronounced dead, and he remained so for a full ninety seconds. But death didn't take. Andy was delirious. "I kept thinking, 'I'm really dead,'" he later recalled. "This is what it's like to be dead—you think you're alive but you're dead. I just think I'm lying here in a hospital.'"

Fifty years later, Valerie shot Andy again. This time, he did die, quickly and without hesitating. Before, there were only boys. Now there was just a girl, and no boys for fifty miles.

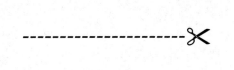

Acknowledgements

Parts of this book were previously presented at Columbia University, Vassar, Ursinus, UC Berkeley, the University of Southern California, and the New School; my thanks to everyone who made those events possible. A short adapted excerpt ran in *New York* magazine.

Between drafts of this book, I underwent major surgery. Recovery was the hardest thing I have ever done, and I owe everything to those who slowly walked my trembling shade out of the Underworld: Brandy, Charlotte, Dayna, Emmett, Harron, Jasmine, Jill, Julie, Kalani, Kate, Marissa, Melissa, Liv, Paisley, Rachael, Sarah, Smaran, Tey, Thora, Torrey, Wendy. My editor at Verso, Jessie Kindig, knew exactly what I needed and made sure I had it. My editor at life, Marissa Brostoff, forced me to say what I was saying. Sarah McCarry held my hand. Charlotte Shane blew in on a wind from the east. And speaking of weather: Sally, you told me never to thank you, and I'm still not listening.

Notes

p. 3 "I'm so female I'm subversive." Valerie Solanas, *Up Your Ass* (unpublished manuscript; Pittsburgh: Andy Warhol Museum Archives, 1965), 18.

p. 3 "Andy *had* lost the play." Breanne Fahs, *Valerie Solanas: The Defiant Life of the Woman Who Wrote SCUM (and Shot Andy Warhol)* (New York: The Feminist Press, 2014), 118–19.

p. 4 "I dedicate this play to ME" . . . "and other degenerates." Solanas, *Up Your Ass*, n.p.

p. 4 "loud, plaid sports jacket." Ibid., 1.

p. 5 "shooting the shit." Fahs, *Valerie Solanas*, 42–44.

pp. 5–6 "The two-sex system" . . . "So has disease." Solanas, *Up Your Ass*, 18.

p. 6 "not physical defects." Valerie Solanas, *SCUM Manifesto* (London: Verso, 2004), 68–69.

p. 6 "The male is a biological accident." Ibid., 35.

p. 6 "to become female." Ibid., 37.

p. 7 "men are women and women are men." Ibid., 38.

p. 7 "'right up' their husbands' assholes." Solanas, *Up Your Ass*, 24.

pp. 7–8 "thrill-seeking female-females." Solanas, *SCUM Manifesto*, 57.

p. 8 "free-wheeling, arrogant females." Ibid., 70.

p. 8 "his maleness" . . . "his femininity." Ibid., 68.

p. 8 "exposing herself." Fahs, *Valerie Solanas*, 69–70.

p. 8 "men who intrude." Solanas, *SCUM Manifesto*, 74.

p. 9 "Give me a kiss." Solanas, *Up Your Ass*, 1.

p. 9 "This reduces me" . . . "little 'feminist' groups." Quoted in Fahs, *Valerie Solanas*, 300.

p. 10 "always selfish" . . . "six-inch blade." Solanas, *SCUM Manifesto*, 76.

p. 11 "Eventually the expression" . . . "a redundancy." Solanas, *Up Your Ass*, 18.

p. 15 "I'm very bitter." Ibid., 12.

p. 15 "Christ almighty." John Logan, *Red* (London: Oberon, 2009), 54.

p. 18 "woman of action." Solanas, *Up Your Ass*, 2.

p. 18 "But it *was* a joke." Maurice Girodias, preface, in *SCUM Manifesto*, Valerie Solanas (New York: Olympia Press, 1970), xi.

p. 19 "incredibly funny." Fahs, *Valerie Solanas*, 34.

p. 19 "Humor is not" . . . "mere 'massive education.'" Quoted in ibid., 35.

p. 19 "It would appear that Miss Solanas." Quoted in ibid., 34.

p. 20 "*SCUM* is the work of the ultimate loser." Vivian Gornick, introduction, in *SCUM Manifesto*, Valerie Solanas (New York: Olympia Press, 1970), xv.

p. 20 "For Valerie, everything was her theories." Quoted in Fahs, *Valerie Solanas*, 153.

p. 22 "see an analyst." Solanas, *Up Your Ass*, 14.

p. 22 "castration complex in women." Sigmund Freud, *The Standard Edition of the Complete Works of Sigmund Freud*, 24 vols, ed. and trans. James Strachey (London: Hogarth Press, 1953–74), 7:195n2.

p. 23 "the little girl is a little man." Freud, *Standard Edition*, 22:118.

p. 24 "envy and jealousy." Ibid., 22:125.

p. 24 "his behavior is approved and hers isn't." Shulamith Firestone, *The Dialectic of Sex: The Case for Feminist Revolution* (New York: Quill, 1970), 57.

p. 24 "still in possession of a penis." Freud, *Standard Edition*, 18:273.

p. 25 "pussy envy." Solanas, *SCUM Manifesto*, 38.

p. 26 "Hell'o, Gorgeous" Solanas, *Up Your Ass*, 1.

p. 26 "Hell'o. Beautiful" . . . "twat by Dior?" Ibid., 1.

p. 26 "original sexual inferiority." Freud, *Standard Edition*, 22:132.

p. 31 "She is" . . . "I've ever run across." Solanas, *Up Your Ass*, 7.

p. 31 "transsexuals rape women's bodies." Janice G. Raymond, *The Transsexual Empire: The Making of the She-Male*, rev. ed. (1979; New York: Teachers College Press, 1994), 104.

p. 31 "one sex-role stereotype for another." Ibid., xvii.

p. 31 "the ultimate" . . . "here possess women." Ibid., 30.

p. 33 "a perfect victim of male suppression." Quoted in Fahs, *Valerie Solanas*, 72.

p. 33 "making fun of women for gay men's entertainment." Ibid., 244.

p. 33 "The male dares" . . . "stilted mannerisms." Solanas, *SCUM Manifesto*, 50–51.

p. 33 "She's so vile" . . . "afternoon mixer." Solanas, *Up Your Ass*, 8.

p. 34 "The male must see" . . . "to the role." Solanas, *SCUM Manifesto*, 51.

p. 35 "You're not too bad-looking" . . . "look like a woman." Solanas, *Up Your Ass*, 12.

p. 36 "Degrading Mindless-Boob-Girlie Symbol." Robin Morgan, "No More Miss America! Ten Points of Protest," in *Sisterhood Is Powerful: An Anthology of Writings from the Women's Liberation Movement*, ed. Robin Morgan (New York: Vintage, 1970), 522.

pp. 36–7 "Each element" . . . " 'like it right away.' " Catharine A. MacKinnon, *Toward a Feminist Theory of the State* (Cambridge: Harvard University Press, 1989), 110.

p. 37 "it is sexuality" . . . "other way around." Ibid., 111.

p. 37 "eroticization of dominance and submission." Ibid., 113.

p. 37 "Man fucks woman; subject verb object." Ibid., 124.

p. 39 "lapping up shit." Solanas, *Up Your Ass*, 10.

p. 39 "It so aptly expresses me." Ibid.,10.

p. 39 "Not to be nosey" . . . "It's for dinner." Ibid., 9.

p. 39 "leading exponent" . . . "labor pains feel good." Ibid., 14–15.

pp. 39–40 "I'm completely attuned" . . . "hours on end." Ibid., 13.

p. 40 "flexible enough" . . . "with equal facility." Ibid., 14.

p. 40 "lost without you." Ibid., 13.

p. 40 "pure feeling" . . . "thought, attitude or idea." Ibid., 11.

p. 40 "Basically [they] told" . . . "Twitter after that." Quoted in Manisha Krishnan, "We Talked to the Woman Who Is Butt Chugging 'Infinite Jest,'" *Vice*, June 15, 2017, vice.com.

p. 41 "I'm not gay" . . . "book, though." "#eatinfinitejest: the first year," YouTube video, June 13, 2017, <youtube.com/watch?v=3eO2QfEGK6U>.

p. 41 "When I'm doing it" . . . "and stay alive." Quoted in Krishnan, "Butt Chugging 'Infinite Jest.'"

p. 42 "I blended together" . . . "it was empty." Quoted in ibid.

pp. 42–3 "Absorbing 'culture'" . . . "they'll ever have." Solanas, *SCUM Manifesto*, 59.

p. 43 "It's a silly thing." Quoted in Krishnan, "Butt Chugging 'Infinite Jest.'"

p. 44 "You don't know" . . . "desexed monstrosity." Solanas, *Up Your Ass*, 18.

p. 45 "social and legal personhood." C. Riley Snorton, *Black on Both Sides: A Racial History of Trans Identity* (Minneapolis: University of Minnesota Press, 2017), 17–53.

pp. 45–6 "As everyone has female" . . . "earlier configuration." "History and Procedure," *MarciBowers.com*, accessed February 16, 2019, <marcibowers.com/mtf/history-procedure>.

pp. 46–7 "If the Adam and Eve story." John Money, *The Adam Principle: Genes, Genitals, Hormones, and Gender: Selected Readings in Sexology* (Buffalo, NY: Prometheus Books, 1993), 56–57.

p. 47 "like a perfect female." Ibid, 57.

p. 47 "macho-minded of males!" Ibid., 57.

p. 48 "I face reality." Solanas, *Up Your Ass*, 8.

p. 49 "Feminism is a political error." Valentine de Saint-Point,

"Manifesto of the Futurist Woman (Response to F. T. Marinetti)," trans. Lawrence Rainey, in *Futurism: An Anthology*, eds Lawrence Rainey, Christine Poggi, and Laura Wittman (New Haven: Yale University Press, 2009), 111.

p. 49 "Every woman must" ... "she is a female." Ibid., 110, translation modified.

p. 52 "Why're *girls* called" ... "the peckers." Solanas, *Up Your Ass*, 2.

p. 52 "Screwing is" ... "to be female." Solanas, *SCUM Manifesto*, 38.

p. 53 "allegory for gender transition." Chelsea L. Shephard, "Call Trans Opt: Transgender Themes in *The Matrix*," *The Ontological Geek* (blog), October 9, 2012, <ontologicalgeek. com/call-trans-opt-transgender-themes-in-the-matrix>.

p. 53 "splinter in your mind." *The Matrix*, dir. Lana and Lily Wachowski (USA: Warner Bros., 1999).

p. 55 "Ignorance is bliss" ... "You understand?" Ibid.

p. 55 "brain and nervous system." Solanas, *SCUM Manifesto*, 68.

p. 55 "vicarious livers" ... "handicapped fellow beings." Ibid., 79.

p. 56 "Come and get it." Solanas, *Up Your Ass*, 19.

p. 56 "complete guide" ... "handling logistics." "HOW TO GET LAID LIKE A WARLORD: 37 Rules of Approaching Model-Tier Girls," Reddit post, November 29, 2016, <reddit. com/r/TheRedPill/comments/5fihmu/how_to_get_laid_ like_a_warlord_37_rules_of>.

p. 57 "*hypergamy*." "Red Pill Jargon and Terminology: A resource for the new and a discussion for the old," Reddit post, September 1, 2014, <reddit.com/r/TheRedPill/ comments/2f841o/red_pill_jargon_and_terminology_a_ resource_for>.

p. 57 "Women want to submit to you." "LIKE A WARLORD."

p. 58 "Women are wired" ... "she'll sleep with you." Ibid.

p. 58 "swim through a river of snot." Solanas, *SCUM Manifesto*, 37.

p. 58 "public relations." Ibid., 38.

p. 59 "He hates his passivity." Ibid., 37.

p. 59 "Good doggie." Solanas, *Up Your Ass*, 19.

p. 59 "gang-rape your girl." "LIKE A WARLORD."

p. 60 "Women will test you brutally" ... "WAR OF ATTRITION." Ibid.

p. 61 "You're too old" ... "off my porch." *Fight Club*, dir. David Fincher (USA: 20th Century Fox, 1999).

p. 61 "how few options" ... "extreme always goes away." Quoted in Ben Beaumont-Thomas, "Fight Club author Chuck Palahniuk on His Book Becoming a Bible for the Incel Movement," *Guardian*, July 20, 2018, theguardian.com.

p. 62 "I star in movies" ... "top directors." Solanas, *Up Your Ass*, 3.

p. 63 "You've fooled your brain." Gavin McInnes, "#NoWanks: How quitting porn and masturbation changed my life," The Rebel, August 14, 2015, therebel.media.

p. 65 "Is there 'feminist' sex? Should there be?" Amber Hollibaugh, "Desire for the Future: Radical Hope in Passion and Pleasure," in *Pleasure and Danger: Exploring Female Sexuality*, ed. Carole S. Vance (Boston: Routledge & Kegan Paul, 1984), 402.

p. 65 "Sex is the refuge" ... "waste of time." Solanas, *SCUM Manifesto*, 60.

p. 65 "SCUM gets around" ... "get to anti-sex." Ibid., 61–62.

p. 65 "Typical male pornography" ... "you want the money." Quoted in Fahs, *Valerie Solanas*, 189.

p. 66 "the romantic in me." Solanas, *Up Your Ass*, 4.

p. 66 "more zestful men's magazines." Ibid., 5.

p. 66 "Why'd you approach me?" ... "ball of fire." Ibid., 3.

p. 68 "fucking losers watch porn" ... "*lose* myself." *Don Jon*, dir. Joseph Gordon-Levitt (USA: Relativity Media, 2013).

p. 69 "more sex with that thing." Ibid.

p. 69 "I do lose myself" ... "lost together." Ibid.

p. 70 "Downright perverse." Solanas, *Up Your Ass*, 26.

p. 71 "About 3 years ago" ... "95 percent sure." "Did sissy porn make me trans or was I trans all a long? (NSFW)" (sic), Reddit post, November 18, 2014, <reddit.com/r/asktransgender/comments /2mn8au>.

p. 72 "Real MTFs don't do that." "Am I a Sissy or MTF? Confused! (Possibly NSFW)," Reddit post, September 2, 2015, <reddit.com /r/asktransgender/comments/3jedmu>.

p. 72 "psychiatrists and clinical psychologists." Solanas, *SCUM Manifesto*, 74.

p. 72 "All gender dysphoric males" . . . "love of oneself as a woman." Ray Blanchard, "The Classification and Labeling of Nonhomosexual Gender Dysphorias," *Archives of Sexual Behavior* 18, no. 4 (1989): 315–34, 322–23.

p. 72–3 "the physical properties of clothing." Ray Blanchard, "Early History of the Concept of Autogynephilia," *Archives of Sexual Behavior* 34, no. 4 (August 2005): 439–46, 441–44.

p. 73 "The term transgender" . . . "sexual fetishism." Sheila Jeffreys, *Gender Hurts: A Feminist Analysis of the Politics of Transgenderism* (London: Routledge, 2014), 14–15.

p. 73 "The use of the term 'sissy' " . . . "degrading and demeaning one." Ibid., 95.

p. 75 "Fuck is in the air." Solanas, *Up Your Ass*, 27.

p. 77 "suicidal ecstasy of being a woman." Leo Bersani, *Is the Rectum a Grave? And Other Essays* (Chicago: University of Chicago Press, 2009), 22.

p. 77 "To call a man" . . . "Surely not pleasure." Solanas, *SCUM Manifesto*, 37.

p. 77 "absent female phallus." Freud, *Standard Edition*, 21:155.

p. 77 "a token of triumph." Ibid., 21:154.

p. 80 "Let the guys ram each other." Solanas, *Up Your Ass*, 26.

p. 80 "two cats, one white and one spade." Ibid., 1

p. 80 "Beat it, Little Boy" . . . "You're perceptive." Ibid., 2.

p. 81 "A white man doesn't stand a chance." Ibid., 3.

p. 82 "infinite virility." Frantz Fanon, *Black Skin, White Masks*, trans. Richard Philcox, rev. ed. (New York: Grove Press, 2008), 123.

p. 84 "hazing rituals." Jane Ward, *Not Gay: Sex Between*

Straight White Men (New York: New York University Press, 2015), 153–90.

p. 85 "Let your soul sway." Solanas, *Up Your Ass*, 15.

p. 86 "I decided to pay attention to brushing my teeth." Allan Kaprow, *Essays on the Blurring of Art and Life*, ed. Jeff Kelley (Berkeley: University of California Press, 1993), 219–20.

p. 90 "probably from emphysema." Fahs, *Valerie Solanas*, 329.

p. 91 "I *am* terrible, aren't I?" Solanas, *Up Your Ass*, 26.

pp. 91–2 "What effect has SCUM had" . . . "Now there are two." Quoted in Fahs, *Valerie Solanas*, 101.

p. 92 "That's not *my* name." Solanas, *Up Your Ass*, 24.

p. 92 "I've tried relating to the emptiness." Ibid., 26.

p. 92–3 "I bet you'd be a crazy lover" . . . "too good a talker." Ibid., 27.

p. 93 "a beautiful, low-down, funky doll." Ibid., 29.

p. 93 "She came right over" . . . "that was that." Quoted in Fahs, *Valerie Solanas*, 105.

pp. 93–4 "I'm a sucker for squishy ass" . . . "the same thing." "I A Man Part 7," YouTube video, February 14, 2009, <youtube.com/watch?v=sPQVtIk3g7s>.

p. 94 "the bullet damaged his stomach." Fahs, *Valerie Solanas*, 141.

p. 94 "I kept thinking." Quoted in ibid., 144–45.